Blessed Is the Man

A Man's Journey through the Psalms

Psalms of Lament

Praise the LORD!
Blessed is the man
who fears the LORD,
who greatly delights
in His commandments!

Psalm 112:1

Copyright © 2010 Concordia Publishing House

3558 S. Jefferson Ave., St. Louis, MO 63118-3968

1-800-325-3040 • www.cph.org

By Joel D. Biermann, Tim Radkey, Tyler Teske, John Shimkus, Steve Sandfort, Gary Dunker, Dave Bangert, and Frank Fischer

Edited by Robert C. Baker

This publication may be available in braille, in large print, or on cassette tape for the visually impaired. Please allow 8 to 12 weeks for delivery. Write to Lutheran Blind Mission, 7550 Watson Rd., St. Louis, MO 63119-4409; call toll free 1-888-215-2455; or visit the Web site: www.blindmission.org.

1 2 3 4 5 6 7 8 9 10   19 18 17 16 15 14 13 12 11 10

Contents

Meet Our Authors

Joel D. Biermann

Joel resides in St. Louis, Missouri, with his bride of twenty-four years, Jeannalee. Their two daughters, Jasmine and Justine, are Lutheran school teachers, and their son Jess is enjoying his formative high school years. Joel's vocation finds him at Concordia Seminary, St. Louis, teaching Systematic Theology. Leading the list of favorite pastimes is any active outdoor pursuit with Jeannalee, who excels at providing what is best for Joel and their family.

Tim Radkey

Tim, his wife, Lea Ann, and their five-year-old daughter, Claire, reside in Lubbock, Texas, where Tim serves as senior pastor of Hope Lutheran Church. Tim has written and appeared in several DVD-based Bible studies produced by LHM's Men's Network. On weekends, Tim and his family enjoy spending time in the mountains of New Mexico. Tim also runs marathons, rides bicycles, and rides around town on his new Harley-Davidson.

Tyler Teske

Tyler lives in Ames, Iowa and is married to Sarah, who is a great encourager, full of laughter, and a wonderful friend. He also is the father of a joyful and exuberant (almost) three-year-old girl. Tyler enjoys eating evening meals with his family, playing outside, and, most recently, tea parties with his daughter. On a less-than-regular basis, Tyler tackles home renovation projects in his 1920's home. He serves as the communications specialist for Iowa State University's Department of Agronomy.

John Shimkus

A graduate of West Point and an Army veteran, John has earned degrees in engineering and business and has two honorary doctorates. A former teacher, he is now serving his thirteenth year in the United States Congress representing the 19th District of Illinois. John and his wife, Karen, have three sons: David, Joshua, and Daniel. They reside in Collinsville, Illinois, where they are active members of Holy Cross Lutheran Church. You can visit John's Web site at shimkus.house.gov.

Frank Fischer

Frank married his high school prom date, who has been his best friend for thirty-one years. Frank and his wife have a daughter, 28, and a son, 26. Frank is a thirty-plus-year veteran of the logistics and supply-chain field and now operates his own third-party logistics enterprise. Frank enjoys fishing, woodworking, singing in the choir, and volunteering to serve our Lord in a variety of capacities at St. John Lutheran Church in Ellisville, Missouri.

Dave Bangert

Dave has been involved in Lutheran education his entire life. Currently, he is executive director of Dallas Lutheran High School. Dave's wife, Jean, is a kindergarten teacher at Our Redeemer Lutheran School, also in Dallas. Dave and Jean have two married sons. Dave enjoys traveling with his wife, working out, reading, and coaching. He has written over 100 devotions for educators. His book, *That They May Have Life*, was published in 2008.

Steve Sandfort

Steve and his wife, Becky, and their three children live in Fort Wayne, Indiana. Following eleven years in church work and eight years as a professional actor and recording artist, Steve has settled into the life of a seminary student at Concordia Theological Seminary. Steve speaks and performs at LCMS events, and he works on film and television when his schedule permits. He and Becky homeschool their children. You can visit Steve at stevesandfort.com.

Gary Dunker

Gary and his wife, Carol, live in Lincoln, Nebraska, where they worship at Messiah Lutheran Church. Gary works in sales for KLCV Radio, a member of the Christian Bott Radio Network. Gary enjoys attending Nebraska football and baseball games, writing adult Bible studies and dramas, as well as spending time with his four grandchildren Evan, Easton, Brynley, and Dathin.

How to Use This Book

This isn't your father's devotional.

Then again, while your father may not have read the stories found in *Blessed Is the Man*, he may have heard stories similar to them. Stories told by his father or brother or friend, real stories from real men who experienced real life relying on God's real—and amazing—grace. Stories like the ones you've heard other believers tell you, or stories you've told yourself.

Blessed Is the Man provides you and your Bible study group with six weeks of faith narratives written by men who have prayerfully considered biblical psalms. At the beginning of each week, you will read an assigned psalm. Five days during that week, you'll read a verse or two of that psalm, followed by the author's story. Next, you may pray a suggested prayer or choose another as you see fit. Finally, you'll answer a few brief Bible study questions, which will help you consider other ways the psalm may apply to you.

To get the most out of *Blessed Is the Man*, prayerfully review the psalm from time to time throughout the week. Through God's Word, the Holy Spirit will confront and challenge, but He will also comfort and console. At the end of each week, join your brothers in Christ in a group Bible study. **Weekly small-group questions are reproducible.** So, if you want to hold your group Bible study before hammering the first nail at a Habitat for Humanity project, at halftime during a televised game, or before you throw the brats on the grill, do so! You may make as many copies of these pages as you need for the guys in your group.

We are grateful that you are taking a man's journey through the Psalms in *Blessed Is the Man*. Along the way, you may be reminded of stories of faith told by your grandfather, father, brother, or friend. The adventure into God's Word may even inspire you to tell a few on your own.

—The Editor

Suggestions for Small-Group Participants

1. Before you begin, spend some time in prayer, asking God to strengthen your faith through a study of His Word. The Scriptures were written so that we might believe in Jesus Christ and have life in His name (John 20:31).

2. Take some time before the meeting to look over the session, review the psalm, and answer the questions.

3. As a courtesy to others, arrive on time.

4. Be an active participant. The leader will guide the group's discussion, not give a lecture.

5. Avoid dominating the conversation by answering every question or by giving unnecessarily long answers. On the other hand, avoid the temptation to not share at all.

6. Treat anything shared in your group as confidential until you have asked for and received permission to share it outside of the group. Treat information about others outside of your group as confidential until you have asked for and received permission to share it with group members.

7. Some participants may be new to Bible study or new to the Christian faith. Help them feel welcome and comfortable.

8. Affirm other participants when you can. If someone offers what you perceive to be a "wrong" answer, ask the Holy Spirit to guide him to seek the correct answer from God's Word.

9. Keep in mind that the questions are discussion starters. Don't be afraid to ask additional questions that relate to the topic. Don't get the group off track.

10. If you are comfortable doing so, volunteer now and then to pray at the beginning or end of the session.

Guide to Men's Ministry

There's a mother watching her boys play in the backyard. The boys are wrestling around in the mud, fighting to see who will be at the top of the pecking order, as brothers often do. There's another mother in the same backyard who has a little girl, or you might even say a *princess*. She comments, "Don't you think those boys are going to hurt one another? How are you going to get the stains out of their clothes?" To this, the mother of the boys replies, "Boys will be boys." In this short story, it is clear that one mother understands boys and the other has no clue how boys become men.

The sad news is this: the Church in many ways has adopted the voice of the princess's mother who never raised boys. It seems men are expected to live, act, and behave in ways that makes sure any remnant of their childhood has been extinguished. Men are tamed to fit the mold of what a good little boy should look like—free of danger, free of risk, and free of anything fun.

Giving men permission to be men once again is absolutely critical to the Church and to a successful men's ministry. There is enough boy left in every man that beckons to compete, have fun, risk, and live out the adventurous spirit only God can give. Yes, it is possible for all of this to happen in the Church while men still live within the will and call of God in their lives.

7 Tips for Men's Ministry

GET "REAL" LEADERS

Men desperately need leaders who are authentic, genuine, and nonjudgmental. You must choose a leader whom other men would want to hang out with and can relate to on multiple levels. This is a guy who other guys love to hang out with because he seems so down to earth, has fun living life, and would be a leader in any environment he found himself in.

THERA-PUKE-IC

Guys need to be in an environment that is natural, not clinical. Guys will share their struggles, challenges, and victories as long as it's not the purpose of the meeting or even the hidden agenda for their time together. When they catch wind that this is about to turn into group therapy, most guys will immediately button their lips, turn off their brain, and look for the nearest exit. When the environment is right, guys will talk. Don't force it. Please, don't force it.

LESS IS MORE

Women are always amazed at how simple men can be at times. Most men like simplicity and are drawn to it. Whether you're planning a men's social, Bible study, retreat, or small group, it is always better to err on the side of keeping it simple. Simple doesn't mean plain or boring; it means doing a few things really, really well. When you sit down to plan activities, try structuring them around broader themes such as having fun, learning a little, and providing a good challenge or risk for men to participate in.

TALKING IS OPTIONAL

Generally when men come together for activities, Bible studies, small groups, and/ or retreats, there is going to be a time for prayer, reading, and answering some questions. There are many men who don't like to read out loud, pray out loud, or be put on the spot to answer questions out loud. Be sure to check with guys ahead of time about praying or reading. There will always be a few men who are comfortable answering questions, and these men usually pave the way for more timid guys to speak up.

KEEP THE SPIRIT OF COMPETITION ALIVE

Not all men played sports, but most men have competed as boys in some area or another. Men, by and large, enjoy competition and friendly wagers. Some men like playing golf against one another, while others enjoy seeing who smokes the best brisket. Either way you slice it, men always enjoy themselves when they can compete in a nonthreatening way, in a way that will never leave them feeling foolish in front of one another.

MEETINGS SHOULD NEVER BE MEETINGS

From time to time, there will be a need to plan various activities for men. The worst thing you can do is form a committee or a board. There will always be natural leaders who will need to do some planning for men's ministry, but have the meeting at a place men enjoy, like an athletic event, a pub, or even on a golf course while playing a round.

No one, especially men, needs to add more "official" meetings to his schedule. Make it informal and fun while you orchestrate real business.

A MINISTRY NEEDS MORE THAN ONE DOOR

How accessible is your ministry? The fastest growing churches always have multiple entry points for folks to get involved and be connected to their church. Men's ministry is no different. While there is a tremendous brotherhood among men, there are also a wide range of things that men like and don't like. Some men like camping and the great outdoors. Other men would prefer manual labor around the church. Some might even like more intellectually oriented activities. No matter what, you need to ensure that your men's ministry has many different attractions that respect different interests, gifts, abilities, and skills. There are venues for all men to come together, and there are activities that will only attract certain men. Keep all these nuances in mind.

3 Steps to Launch a Men's Ministry in *Your* Church

LOCATION, LOCATION, LOCATION

Pick a place that will work for launching your first men's ministry event. A tail-gate setting would be an absolutely prime site. Other options are at a lake, the rustic outdoors, or even a barn of sorts. Whatever you choose as your site, it should be a place where guys can get excited and loud and not feel closed in.

MEN EAT MEAT AND LOTS OF IT

Once you've got the location nailed down, it's time to think about the meat you are going to serve. Depending on what area of the country you live in, your choices and preferences will vary. Some examples are having a wild-game type spread of food. This usually takes place in areas where men enjoy hunting. If you have chosen a tailgate at some sporting event, cook up a bunch of bratwurst, brisket, and/or ribs. Warning: it's tough to cook a great steak when you're doing it in large numbers. Men are picky with their steaks, so be careful if this is your choice. Don't forget to bring beverages that your men would enjoy as well. (Okay, you can throw on some veggie burgers too.)

IT'S TIME TO LAUNCH—THE DAY IS HERE

Okay, you've chosen a great site. You've got the volunteers you need to cook the meat at the site. Now it's time to plan how you are going to effectively brainstorm what your men's ministry might look like. This is not a time to be critical of ideas. This is a time to really listen to what men are saying.

- What kinds of activities do they want to be involved with?

- What kinds of adventures are they looking for?

- What contribution do they want their men's ministry to make to the kingdom of God externally and their church internally?

Make this fun. For example, to get things started you could have some balloons attached to a big piece of plywood and have various ideas written on paper inside of the balloons. Have one of the men use the BB gun you provided to shoot one of the balloons and see what idea is inside and talk about it. This exercise can be a lot of fun, but please be safe with it. Once you have some good ideas about the direction the men would like to go, pick another location to flesh out more of the details and planning. Ask for any volunteers who want to help with this next phase. Once this next phase is finished, you should be able to get to work—but don't forget to keep on listening to the men in your church.

Introduction

There's nothing worse than a whiner. Most of us would agree that it's not good when someone adopts the whole "victimhood" thing and begins to plead for special consideration or rights because he has been made a "victim." And you know that backseat groaning about the length of a road trip—even those delivered in a rare spirit of self-control and rationality—can wear down the most patient parent. Listening to your neighbor retrace the Möbius-strip-litany of his personal health problems strains the most altruistic attempt at unconditional love. Any of these events is capable of severely challenging your virtuous intention of extending love, compassion, and concern to those in need. Taken by themselves, these scenarios are bad enough; but any one of these situations, and countless others like them, become infinitely more difficult to negotiate when they are delivered with a whine. Indeed, even an uplifting and positive word can be perverted into a grating malediction when spoken with a whine. "You're the best!" and "I love you" sound like curses when they are not spoken but whined.

The validity of the argument just made could generate some grave doubts about the project about to be undertaken in the volume you now hold. This is a study guide for individual and group use based on the psalms, of course. But the psalms selected for inclusion in this study were not gathered at random. They share at least one common and governing characteristic. Interestingly, not one of the six psalms gathered here came from the pen of the most famous psalmist. None are Davidic. But that's not why they were selected. They were collected on the basis of topic.

The various authors of the psalms took up a variety of topics as they composed Israel's songbook. Previous volumes in this series focused on two of these topics: wisdom psalms (vol. 1) and messianic psalms (vol. 2). This volume takes up a third grouping—one that may be the most difficult to interpret but is perhaps the most meaningful and relevant: psalms of lament. This study will consider six psalms that, if read with the wrong tone, may actually begin to sound like whining! And that, of course, is a bit of a problem. Only a fool would try to construe whining as somehow virtuous; but only a greater fool would suggest that a part of Holy Scripture is in some way unsavory or even deficient! It is necessary, then, to come to terms with what is going on in these psalms of lament, and to find some way to appreciate and appropriate their message without mistakenly hearing it as merely complaining at best and whining at worst.

To begin, it is worth remembering that the people of Israel did face some genuinely daunting and terrifying threats. Politically and nationally, the sovereignty of their struggling monarchy was frequently imperiled by their immediate neighbors, who had no great love for the former Egyptian slaves and who saw them as little more than invaders and squatters. But these local pressures paled in comparison to the looming storm that was building in Mesopotamia. Assyria was rising to prominence and would bring Judah to its knees and Israel to utter ruin. Given the people's situation, wrenching fear bordering on panic was *not* out of order. More important, though, is the need to recognize that these psalms are the prayers of God's people at the time of acute need. What you will read and study in these psalms of lament are the heartfelt pleas of people who knew God as their only Savior and their only hope in the face of the most severe crisis—a crisis that was not only political but also spiritual. Recall that the nations surrounding Israel all confessed false gods and assumed that military and diplomatic conquest and success was a certain sign of their national deity's supremacy. The people of Israel, especially those who led Israel in their corporate worship and prayers, were justified in giving plaintive voice to the desperate need of the nation.

Above all, it is critical to appreciate the nature of these psalms not as dispassionate corporate prayers, much less as carefully formulated doctrinal expositions about God's providence or hiddeness—as the case may be. These prayers are the record of a people facing disgrace, defeat, and national annihilation and so pleading with their only hope to come to their aid. Twenty-first-century readers do well to read these prayers with a sense of holy reverence, rather than one of detached disinterest or critical evaluation. In other words, do not make the sad mistake of treating these psalms like a depository of eternal propositions waiting to be mined and brought into the bright light of day by you, the brilliant expositor. Do not scan these psalms looking for "insights" into your own life or into the character of God. This is not to say that such insights may not be encountered during the study of these selected psalms, but the hunt for insights misses the true beauty and significance of these psalms. The real power of these psalms is their ability to articulate the believer's anguish of heart and soul as he wrestles with the difficulty of believing in an omnipotent God who loves profoundly, while at the same time living in a world that appears to defy this God and His commandments yet without consequence. These psalms are about life as it is lived and experienced; accordingly, they also should be lived and experienced and not merely studied or mined. The best way to read the psalms is to enter into them with the psalmist and to use his words to recount your own inner struggles and to vocalize your own fervent prayers for God to intervene. These are psalms not just about ancient Israel and her understanding of God, but about real life, today.

Using these psalms of lament as one's own personal prayer book raises a question of significance and relevance. There is no question about the significance and relevance of the psalmists' words, but there is a legitimate question about whether the challenges and difficulties typically faced by today's readers rise to the level of the problems besetting the psalms' authors. To be blunt: do the petty problems we routinely encounter deserve to be considered with the sort of trials motivating the psalmists? We lose wallets, opportunities, jobs, self-respect, and our temper; Israel's people were threatened with losing their nation, homes, children, existence, and faith. Is there really a comparison? Do we demean the psalms by using them to help us handle our mundane and trivial trials? In our narcissistic culture, it must be stressed that the tendency to overestimate the importance of ourselves and our own lives, problems, and pain must be repudiated and confessed as sin. We are, as a rule, far too full of ourselves and far too little appreciative of the plight of others—even ancient brothers in the faith. It is arrogant and foolish to lump our discomforts and inconveniences with the agony of soul endured by those who penned these psalms—as well as with our contemporaries who endure much for the name of Christ. There is no comparison. On the other hand, we must also be wary of underestimating the eternal issues that hang in the balance when we make decisions about how we will handle the endless stream of annoyances and provocations that afflict us in our daily lives. God uses even the trivial stuff of routine living to work His purposes in our lives. So, while you may feel a bit sheepish about using one of these psalms to pray about what many would consider to be of no consequence, it is good to be reminded that as far as God is concerned, it all matters; and learning to see little problems in the right way can be excellent practice for life's inevitable bigger challenges.

Before delving into the texts themselves, consider one last item. You will quickly note that while these psalms are lumped under the category of lament, they often readily morph into another more troubling category with the intimidating title of imprecatory psalms. Imprecatory passages are typically glossed over in embarrassment, calling as they do for God to bring shame, harsh judgment, and merciless destruction on the unfortunate enemies of Israel. To the modern Christian reader, these words seem woefully out of place—unworthy of the loving Gospel-motivated attitude that should characterize our dealings with those who make themselves our enemies. It must be remembered, however, that along with mercy, justice *is* also an attribute of our Lord. And the extension of justice means vindication of the downtrodden and punishment of the rebellious and wicked. This truth extends even into the New Testament and is seen, for example, in many of Jesus' parables. So, while we indeed love our enemies and pray God to show them His mercy, there yet remains a place for the cry for justice—even with its sad but necessary consequences.

Perhaps your heart is light today, and psalms of lament seem somehow inappropriate. Press forward anyway. You know that your day of sorrow will come. And for the

Christian, it is profoundly true that every day should be marked with the lament of the sinner who knows the truth about himself and pleads to God for the mercy he does not deserve but desperately needs. Broken and desperate is always the best place for a Christian to be, because it is then that God delivers His grace. It is then that He gives Christ.

Week One

Psalm 44

[1] O God, we have heard with our ears,
our fathers have told us,
what deeds You performed in their days,
in the days of old:

[2] You with Your own hand drove out the nations,
but them You planted;
You afflicted the peoples,
but them You set free;

[3] for not by their own sword did they win the land,
nor did their own arm save them,
but Your right hand and Your arm,
and the light of Your face,
for You delighted in them.

[4] You are my King, O God;
ordain salvation for Jacob!

[5] Through You we push down our foes;
through Your name we tread down
those who rise up against us.

[6] For not in my bow do I trust,
nor can my sword save me.

[7] But You have saved us from our foes
and have put to shame those who hate us.

[8] In God we have boasted continually,
and we will give thanks to Your name forever. *Selah*

⁹ But You have rejected us and disgraced us
and have not gone out with our armies.

¹⁰ You have made us turn back from the foe,
and those who hate us have gotten spoil.

¹¹ You have made us like sheep for slaughter
and have scattered us among the nations.

¹² You have sold Your people for a trifle,
demanding no high price for them.

¹³ You have made us the taunt of our neighbors,
the derision and scorn of those around us.

¹⁴ You have made us a byword among the nations,
a laughingstock among the peoples.

¹⁵ All day long my disgrace is before me,
and shame has covered my face

¹⁶ at the sound of the taunter and reviler,
at the sight of the enemy and the avenger.

¹⁷ All this has come upon us,
though we have not forgotten You,
and we have not been false to Your covenant.

¹⁸ Our heart has not turned back,
nor have our steps departed from Your way;

¹⁹ yet You have broken us in the place of jackals
and covered us with the shadow of death.

²⁰ If we had forgotten the name of our God
or spread out our hands to a foreign god,

²¹ would not God discover this?
For He knows the secrets of the heart.

²² Yet for Your sake we are killed all the day long;
we are regarded as sheep to be slaughtered.

²³ Awake! Why are You sleeping, O Lord?
Rouse Yourself! Do not reject us forever!

²⁴ Why do You hide Your face?
Why do You forget our affliction and oppression?

²⁵ For our soul is bowed down to the dust;
our belly clings to the ground.

²⁶ Rise up; come to our help!
Redeem us for the sake of Your steadfast love!

Tyler Teske

Psalm 44:1-3

O God, we have heard with our ears, our fathers have told us, what deeds You performed in their days, in the days of old: You with Your own hand drove out the nations, but them You planted; You afflicted the peoples, but them You set free; for not by their own sword did they win the land, nor did their own arm save them, but Your right hand and Your arm, and the light of Your face, for You delighted in them.

Talk to Me

I often think of God as "showing off" in the Old Testament. Sometimes I long for God to act like He oftentimes did then, to hang out like He did when the Israelites wandered around in the wilderness. A pillar of cloud by day, a pillar of fire by night. Fire that consumes a soaking wet altar. A huge body of water that parts in the middle. A city that crumbles to pieces at the sound of trumpets. A God who wipes out my enemies.

But, upon further exploration, even in those days God's presence in fire, thunder, and lightning was pretty uncommon. God tended to interact with His people in a different way—sometimes through an angelic messenger, oftentimes through a human being. Usually, God talked to His people through His prophets or some other special servant, and that servant conveyed God's messages. Thinking about it further, the people of the Old Testament often displayed a lot of trust. Fire from heaven was rare. What was more common was God's prophets speaking or writing God's Word, a Word His people trusted.

The author of Psalm 44 is thinking about past conquests of his ancestors. God would tell His messenger to take on a particular battle and the people would be victorious. When Joshua marched around Jericho, or when Gideon defeated an army of tens of thousands with three hundred men, the people listened to God and trusted in Him. When we see God's hand at work in overcoming an obstacle or enemy, listening to God and trusting what He says is what should come first.

Unfortunately, I find listening to God and trusting His Word to be very difficult. There are so many examples of God talking to people in the Old Testament—Moses, Abraham, Gideon, Elijah and the prophets—and I often wonder exactly how the prophets conversed with God. If He sometimes spoke to them in dreams, did they dream about talking to Him? Or, did they talk out loud? How exactly did that work? I find myself wanting God to call out my name in the night or put on some sort of showy display.

Instead, God is much more subtle, like the small still voice talking on the mountain to Elijah. Or, in my case, the calm, quiet voice that spoke to me in the shower.

Perhaps this sounds a little odd, but it's true. I've never really mentioned it to anyone before so this could be a common experience for people that I would never know about. Regardless, when the water starts flowing in the morning, it isn't uncommon for me to speak to God, to pray to Him. Usually I talk about how I should be viewing a conflict I am having with someone, or why I am struggling with a project, or how to accomplish my long list of tasks, or sometimes (by which I mean almost always) I talk to Him about how I am living my life.

Mostly, God listens. He is very quiet and an excellent listener. But, occasionally, God speaks. By that I mean He works through His Word so that I understand and apply it to my life. Recently I found myself facing the front wall of the shower, water running down over my head, my heart in a very calm and still place. God was making His point and I was listening: If you really think your faith is important, why don't you write about it? Ouch. Here's a different translation: "I gave you the gift of words to help people learn and understand. Because this is a God-given gift, you should use it for Me." I stood there for at least a couple of minutes praying about that and talking with God.

We don't get a lot of details on how the prophets talked to God, but we do see how Jesus did it. Jesus frequently went off by Himself to pray. He cleared out the clutter and distractions and dedicated His time and energy to focus on talking to God the Father. Jesus' example is pretty stunning if you look through the Gospels for it. Unfortunately, I am much more like the dimwitted disciples who busied themselves with the things of the world, became overwhelmed by all the people who were interested in listening to Jesus, and couldn't ever quite grasp what was going on. Jesus went off to pray by Himself and the disciples never seemed to follow Jesus' lead. And I am guilty of the same.

Fortunately, God is patient. He doesn't ask me to be perfect; He simply asks me to listen. And, just as when He appeared daily to the Israelites as a pillar of cloud or fire, He asks me to follow His lead. Instead of being discouraged because the world doesn't seem like it was in the time of the prophets, I can be encouraged that God still speaks to us through His Word. Yes, even in a shower.

I would be remiss if I didn't mention that God also speaks to me through other people. Luther called it the "mutual conversation" of Christians. It is a different sort of voice than those morning moments in the shower. And it is certainly more frequent. Most often, God talks to me through my wife. I have been blessed with a mate who has a heart that burns with the Holy Spirit and is filled with a longing to grow spiritually. My own fire can sometimes be small and cold. But she is there to remind me, encourage me, and fan the flames of faith.

And God is there throughout my daily life. On Sundays, God speaks to me through His Word, the sermon, and the hymns. Jesus reaches out in bread and wine and touches me with His flesh and blood. And God places Christians all around me during the week. There are so many little ways God is speaking to me; if I but pay attention and listen, it is really hard *not* to hear God in my daily life. Our loving, patient, forgiving, and comforting God, who saved us through His right hand and arm (v. 3), Jesus Christ, actively pursues us so that we learn to listen. Suddenly, it isn't so difficult to imagine how the prophets heard the voice of God.

There are so many little ways God is speaking to me; if I but pay attention and listen, it is really hard *not* to hear God in my daily life.

Prayer: Lord God, there are many things in my life vying for my attention. Help me daily to make time so that I can hear You speak to me in Your Word and respond to You in prayer, praise, and godly living. I ask this through Christ, my Lord. Amen.

Monday

Daily Study Questions
Psalm 44:1–3

1. Recall a situation when you were quite sure that God was telling you something—how did you know it was God who was "speaking"?

2. What does the psalmist mean by the "days of old"?

3. Why were those days so significant for the psalmist even centuries later?

4. Why is it important to recall that miracles were not part of the regular routine of life in "Bible times"?

5. What are the stories that you need to be speaking into the ears of those around you, especially into the ears of the next generation of God's people?

Psalm 44:4-8

You are my King, O God; ordain salvation for Jacob! Through You we push down our foes; through Your name we tread down those who rise up against us. For not in my bow do I trust, nor can my sword save me. But You have saved us from our foes and have put to shame those who hate us. In God we have boasted continually, and we will give thanks to Your name forever. *Selah*

It Wasn't Me

There are few things in life as rewarding and inspiring as a story well told. Maybe I'm biased as someone employed in the communications field, but when I see a movie in the theater that creates a stir, generates huge crowds, and makes people start talking, something tells me it isn't simply due to pretty pictures. Movies that win multiple Oscars and garner rave reviews have something to say about relationships, about people, and about the human condition.

The most inspiring seem to be stories of conquest, the victory against all odds that leaves the hero triumphant. This sort of story is rampant in the Old Testament—God drives out the nations and plants His people. Woo-hoo! Stick it to them! We win! Teach those bad guys a lesson.

But somehow it is always different with God than it is in the movies. While the stories in books and on the big screen seem to always glorify the victor, we often see in Scripture the frailty and impossibility of any sort of triumph on human terms. While movies and books can strike a chord with us, real life delivers something much less neat and tidy. And that oftentimes is good.

I'm not sure how my life would work as a movie. It sometimes *feels* dramatic. I am part of the statistic claiming the average American worker will have three to five careers and ten to twelve different jobs before retirement. I didn't believe this when I graduated with my bachelor's degree. But God certainly has been showing me the ins and outs of those statistics. In fewer than ten years, I am already working for my third employer and have changed career paths twice. Unlike some of my friends, though, my employment moves haven't exactly been of my own volition. Losing or changing jobs is a huge lesson in trust and patience.

I can't help but think that the Hebrews leaving Egypt probably had similar feelings. Or the warriors marching around Jericho. Or the disciples heading out to spread the Good News of Christ.

But there *is* a major upside to being displaced from the familiar and heading forth into the unknown—the possible realization that the only available source of help is God.

My first post-college employment experience was a dream job. I was one of five producer-directors for a nationally syndicated public television program, I assumed the role of Web-site coordinator, and I was able to play with technology, which had the added bonus of making our production group much more efficient. This, of course, ended. And without so much as a lead from any prospective employers.

I'll kill some of the suspense here and say that God was kind and I was off the unemployment rolls in less than a month. But still, it was a stressful time. I kept reminding myself that, while I needed to keep working to find employment, God would provide what I needed in His time. It turned out that within a couple days of losing my job I suddenly had two possibilities—one in the communications field, the other in financial services. After a lot of prayer, I decided to get out of my comfort zone and take a crack at commission sales.

The big hurdle facing me was the subject matter. To gain a license to sell investments, I was required to take one of the toughest tests on the planet, the Series 7. I have no doubt in my mind that God uses huge obstacles in my life to help me focus on Christ. And this wasn't just a boulder, it was a mountain.

The psalmist in today's reading talks about God providing the victory, not the bows and swords we use in battle. The ability to see God's hand at work in any situation is a wonderful skill. Of course, God's hand is quite obvious when revisiting events such as the Israelites walking on dry land as they cross the Red Sea. It is much less obvious in the small battles and feats of human strength. I can very quickly be lulled into thinking that my accomplishments are my own. But when I stop and pray, it becomes very clear to me how vast and expansive a role God plays in my everyday life.

Luckily for me, the Series 7 was so completely outside the realm of my experience that I had no choice but to look to God for help. I was eager to learn and willing to work hard, but I also was just as eager to have God as an integral part of the process. I abandoned my typically "lean on God" mentality and crawled right up into His hands. No sense in pretending.

It was fortunate that I was unemployed when I began to prepare for the test. Studying became my full-time job. I read the training materials, attended a week-long class with evening homework, reread everything, and then spent an entire week taking practice tests. I never used to understand what Paul meant when he said to "pray without ceasing" (1 Thessalonians 5:7) until that point.

To pass the test, you needed to score 70 percent. I scored better than 90. That might sound like bragging, but I never felt like it was my personal accomplishment. I simply got on for the ride and let God guide the tools.

The psalmist captures that same perspective in today's reading. It wasn't the sword or the strength of the army that gave them victory; it was God's strength and His love for His people. And we see this same pattern repeated again and again—God conquers Pharaoh; God conquers Canaan; God conquers Jericho. Ultimately, the pattern culminates in Christ's death and resurrection. What a great joy to be able to say, "O death, where is your victory? O death, where is your sting?" (1 Corinthians 15:55). All because of God's love and strength, which we see most clearly in Christ's cross and now-empty tomb, we see victory in a challenge we could never face ourselves.

In light of what Christ accomplished for me, I have a new challenge—to remember God's love and strength are there every moment of every day. To know that when I tackle a life-changing test or simply interact with my wife and child, I can let God guide the tools and revel in his love. God's love is so much better than my strength. I love His victories.

....

The psalmist captures that same perspective in today's reading. It wasn't the sword or the strength of the army that gave them victory; it was God's strength and His love for His people.

Prayer: Heavenly Father, all of the victories in my life belong to You. Help me not to boast in my skills and abilities, but to boast about You and what You have accomplished for me and the whole world through Your Son, Jesus Christ. In His name I pray. Amen.

....

Tuesday

Daily Study Questions
Psalm 44:4–8

1. Think of a time that God provided a victory in your life when most people would have declared the situation hopeless. Must these victories always appear miraculous?

2. If the psalmist is part of the Davidic kingdom of Jacob (with a very human king ruling over him), how is he able to declare that God is his king?

3. If God does the fighting and the victory is His alone, then why do we even bother to have a bow or sword?

4. Are there actually people who hate you, or was this a complaint unique to the psalmist?

5. What challenges are you facing today that could be better met by following the psalmist's example of finally trusting in God to bring a victory that you worked hard to win?

Psalm 44:9–16

But You have rejected us and disgraced us and have not gone out with our armies. You have made us turn back from the foe, and those who hate us have gotten spoil. You have made us like sheep for slaughter and have scattered us among the nations. You have sold Your people for a trifle, demanding no high price for them. You have made us the taunt of our neighbors, the derision and scorn of those around us. You have made us a byword among the nations, a laughingstock among the peoples. All day long my disgrace is before me, and shame has covered my face at the sound of the taunter and reviler, at the sight of the enemy and the avenger.

Perspective

When I was a sophomore in college, I took part in what I am pretty sure was one of the most demanding sports-conditioning drills known to man. It was simply called "the hills." The drill was a result of the opportunity I had to play soccer at the college level, which made me "fortunate" enough to condition and practice at the college level.

It was small-college ball, but definitely a much more advanced level than my previous experience in every aspect. We started the season in the middle of August with "three-a-days," three practice sessions per day for the first week. And because most of us weren't disciplined enough to work out on our own during our summer break, most of the practices were dedicated to conditioning. "You may not be the most talented group of players," said Coach, "but no one will be in better physical condition than this team."

Coach had us in constant motion. He made sure we occupied our down time with a constant rotation of exercises: the dead cockroach, push-ups, and crunches. He had us doing three-mile runs. We were losing weight we didn't know we could lose. But the undeniable king of all the conditioning drills was running hills.

The college where I played had practice fields on top of what amounted to a plateau. The sides were steep. I might be underestimating the grade at 40 percent. And the hill was around 75 feet long. If you stood at the bottom and drop-kicked a ball really well, the ball would land on top of the hill at the high point of the arc of the kick; usually it would roll back down to you. The hill was a formidable opponent to run up.

The drill was brutal; by the third day, the hill had become an ominous beast. Every time we ran the drill, a few more people fell behind while the others struggled to stay in step. Coach decided that some of us weren't putting out enough effort and started making us run the hill until *everyone* had scaled it fifteen times.

It was the middle of the afternoon in the middle of August in Nebraska. Fiendishly hot. Some players were frustrated that they would need to continue to scale that beast while waiting for others to finish. Someone fired off a derogatory remark toward the slower players. A few others joined in.

"Let's add another hill," Coach called out.

Someone else testified to how the slower runners were bringing everyone down.

"There's another lap. Anyone else want to add their comments?" bellowed Coach.

It was tough enough for me to bust my tail up and down that monstrous slope, gutting it out, hardening myself mentally by repeating endlessly, "Keep moving. You can do it. You get a break on the way down. One more. One more." But I was in reasonably good shape; I had a long stride and could generally keep up with the rest of the players. For those few who were losing the physical and mental battle with the hill and then running the gauntlet of degrading insults, it must have been totally crushing. It would have been hard not to feel worthless at that moment.

> All day long my disgrace is before me, and shame has covered my face at the sound of the taunter and reviler, at the sight of the enemy and the avenger. (vv. 15–16)

I've never faced the headlong assaults on my faith that I hear goes on in places such as Indonesia and Eastern Africa. I truly have no idea what that is like. I have never feared for my life as a result of my faith in Jesus. But I do know that our world is difficult to live in as a Christian, and often it is truly brutal. For me, the common sort of persecution is the thousand-paper-cuts style of attack, the hundreds of little influences that work to erode my faith. Satan is always waiting for a distracted or weak moment to drop the seeds of doubt. "Look at your crappy life. You are a loser. No one loves you. You're weak—a lazy father; a poor husband; an ungrateful son; an uncaring friend; alone. You're not even a good Christian. It's not worth it. Why would God listen to you? Just keep quiet. No one cares. You are worthless."

Satan is always trying to lead us to that last phrase: you are worthless.

That would be an easy place to end up without Christ. But Jesus' defeat of sin, Satan, and death on the cross took place for all of us. Which means that we aren't worthless; we are priceless. God loves us so much that He paid the only possible price for us to make us part of His family: the precious blood of Jesus, His Son (see 1 Corinthians 6:20; Ephesians 2:12–13; 1 John 1:7).

Then, Jesus says, "In the world you will have tribulation. But take heart; I have overcome the world" (John 16:33). He sets our expectations and states the facts clearly: "Your road won't be easy, but I have defeated death. What harm can come to you?" Christ promises that we are never alone, He is with us always "to the end of the age" (Matthew 28:20). As if that weren't enough, God sends us other Christians to build us up in the faith and encourage us on our way—you know, family members, brothers and sisters in Christ.

After Coach "rewarded" that second round of disparaging remarks, it took only one more trip up the hill before the phrases of encouragement started to echo: "Keep it up!" "Here we go." "You've got it, man." "Let's go!" Out of breath, sweating like mules, and with legs and lungs on fire, we pushed ourselves to make sure our team-mates completed their task. As we passed our teammates, we gave them the best boost of confidence we could. We cheered them on. Suddenly, they weren't the out-casts. They belonged to us. We were all a part of the team.

In the end, those slower hill runners never became our star athletes. I'm not even sure if they all actually played in competition. I do know that without them we may not have become a team. Their worth wasn't measured in goals and playing time. God gave us those teammates to make us a team.

In the midst of derision and turmoil, Christ tells us that we belong to Him. We hear it in a Sunday service. We hear it from our wives or other family members. We hear it from co-workers who are of the household of faith. We're not worthless out-casts of Satan's lies. We, you and I, are children of God.

Jesus' defeat of sin, Satan, and death on the cross took place for all of us. Which means that we aren't worthless; we are priceless.

Prayer: Dear Lord, You discipline me in love because I am Your child. Help me to know that such discipline is for my good, and help me to trust in Your gracious promises in Your Word. In Jesus' name. Amen.

Wednesday

1. Remember a time when some challenge or crushing defeat forced you to contemplate the degree of your own personal worthlessness. What specifically made the experience so difficult to bear?

2. We typically associate good things and blessings with God's action but credit the pain and setbacks with the work of Satan, the adversary. How does the psalmist challenge this easy formula?

3. In verses 4–8 and 9–16, is the psalmist describing two different groups of people or the same group on different days; or is there another explanation for the dramatic shift in the tone of the psalm?

4. Have you ever experienced the derision and mocking of those who are enemies of God's truth? Why would God allow His own name to become a source of reproach among the people of the world?

5. Today's message is heavy on the Law—where does it leave you emotionally and spiritually?

Psalm 44:17-22

All this has come upon us, though we have not forgotten You, and we have not been false to Your covenant. Our heart has not turned back, nor have our steps departed from Your way; yet You have broken us in the place of jackals and covered us with the shadow of death. If we had forgotten the name of our God or spread out our hands to a foreign god, would not God discover this? For He knows the secrets of the heart. Yet for Your sake we are killed all the day long; we are regarded as sheep to be slaughtered.

What Were They Thinking?

I sometimes think the psalmists are kind of whiny. Maybe that is a bit unfair because I have the advantage of believing in Christ after His death and resurrection. But it still makes me wonder sometimes what the writers were thinking.

It's obvious from reading through the Old Testament what the Israelites thought should happen. They thought they should be always victorious in battle, never under the rule of another nation, impenetrable to siege, blessed endlessly with earthly things, respected by others, and a shining star to the world around them. Seriously, whose life is like that? Did these writers know anyone who fit that description?

Of course, I would be remiss if I said I never think this way. I would equate the prayers I prayed in elementary and middle school to this similar tone and mindset. Actually, the prayers from my last job change just a short time ago weren't too far off, either. Certainly, the deep anguish, if not the language, were very similar to verses 17–22 in Psalm 44. I never recall using the terms "shadow of death" and "sheep to be slaughtered"; I'm not that melodramatic. But "crushed" and "deep darkness" certainly come to mind.

After four years of being self-employed selling insurance and investments, the situation had become much less than ideal. I am positive my wife knew this much earlier than I did. The job required me to work long hours and we were entirely dependent on commissions from the products I sold. My absence also meant my wife was getting no break from her full-time job of being a mom. We had a very young baby, and we knew my absence would soon have significant negative effects on her. The sporadic and wildly fluctuating income was becoming problematic. After some long conversations with my wife, I acknowledged the obvious need for change. Our lives needed to be different to allow our family to function properly and do what God wanted for the three of us. That was in March.

What followed were late nights as my wife and I worked on my resumé after I came home from work. Then more late nights as we put my job applications in order. I was taking time occasionally during the day to write cover letters or look for job postings.

As time wore on, the income situation became worse—we started sliding quickly backward. Looking for a job when you are self-employed is not ideal. My first interview was in late June. After a lot of waiting, that position was offered to someone else. It was getting dark.

August arrived. More resumés and cover letters. More debt. A major rewrite of my resumé. More debt. A possible lead on a job opening at the local university. More waiting. It took weeks for that lead to materialize. Then I was advised by someone close to that position to look at some other options. October rolled around and the emotional, financial, and relational strains were not just palpable but ever-present.

Somewhere in there, a couple of times, my wife had just about had it. She was near the end of her rope. We were both beginning to feel as though we were living aspects of this psalm. It was definitely a dark place.

The good part about being in such a dark place is that you notice how near God is—it's hard to miss Him when you are constantly in prayer. I was praying continually, fervently, and with a groaning heart. The bad part was that we were still in that dark place.

> All this has come upon us, though we have not forgotten You, and we have not been false to Your covenant. Our heart has not turned back, nor have our steps departed from Your way. (vv. 17–18)

I tried desperately to be encouraging to my wife. I also tried desperately to steer away from asking God, "Why is this happening?" But I still had plenty of moments of despair. We each questioned whether we were doing something to make God mad. It was hard not to feel like we were being hung out to dry.

As I wrestled with all of this in prayer, God kept steering me back to focus on what He really wants for our family and the reason why we started the process in the first place. And I found myself clinging to God's promises: "In the world you will have tribulation. But take heart; I [Jesus] have overcome the world" (John 16:33); "And we know that for those who love God all things work together for good, for those who are called according to His purpose" (Romans 8:28). Despite that, I was emotionally gutted and I laid it all out on God.

In the last weeks of October, I received a phone call to interview with one of the departments at the local university. I was shocked. To my recollection, the application process had closed almost two months prior. This new interview went well, the position looked to be a great fit for me, and I felt I could really enjoy working with the people in that department. Then I waited again.

It was another two months before that interview materialized into employment, but that day in mid-December marked the end of the dark time. Despite still having plenty of lingering effects from my past employment, the road ahead was much less dim.

That isn't really the end of the story. I didn't realize the full benefit of landing where I did until the collapse of the financial markets hit roughly nine months later. While the state was slashing funds from university budgets, the funding source for my position was largely insulated from such economic events. The long, dark time suddenly seemed a lot less long and dark.

God reminds us that life isn't easy and that there will be dark times. But He promises to never leave our side. He promises love and forgiveness and salvation. He promises that Jesus' sacrifice on the cross did it all. And He promises that *all* times, good or dark, belong to Him, and that we can always trust Him. I'm sure, in the midst of his darkness, that that was what the psalmist was thinking. It certainly was what Paul was thinking when he quoted verse 22 in Romans 8:36. To that he added, just two verses later,

> For I am sure that neither death nor life, nor angels nor rulers, nor things present nor things to come, nor powers, nor height nor depth, nor anything else in all creation, will be able to separate us from the love of God in Christ Jesus our Lord. (Romans 8:38–39)

God reminds us that life isn't easy and that there will be dark times. But He promises to never leave our side. He promises love and forgiveness and salvation.

Prayer: Lord Jesus, sometimes I feel broken and in the shadows. Mend my body and spirit, and shine the light of Your grace into my life by Your Word. Let me know and feel God's love through You. I ask this in Your name. Amen.

Thursday

1. What's the darkest season that you have been through in the last couple of years?

2. Did living through this particular dark time cause you to experience God's special presence or His absence?

3. What is particularly distressing to the psalmist as he goes through the challenging season with the rest of his countrymen?

4. In what sense does God's omniscience pose a particular difficulty for the Christian counting on God to make "all things work together for good" (Roman 8:28)?

5. How does the sober reality of the Christian life, as marked by suffering and difficulty (so pointedly and honestly declared by the psalmist), shape the way that you approach the coming day?

Psalm 44:23-26

Awake! Why are you sleeping, O Lord? Rouse Yourself! Do not reject us forever! Why do You hide Your face? Why do You forget our affliction and oppression? For our soul is bowed down to the dust; our belly clings to the ground. Rise up; come to our help! Redeem us for the sake of Your steadfast love!

The Next Stage

I'm not entirely sure at what age I started looking forward to what I called "the next stage." When I was in elementary school, that next stage was middle school. When I was in middle school, that next stage was high school. When I was in high school, that next stage was college. On a yearly basis, the next stage was summer camp or a winter retreat. I always had something to look forward to.

If I had been a popular kid in school, perhaps I wouldn't have longed so fervently for the next stage. But I was a little bit geeky, a little bit gangly, and a little too talkative. And sometimes I was just plain weird, even by my standards. All of those things mean I was verbally picked on a little. At the time, it seemed as though I was harassed constantly (though, looking back, I think "sometimes" would be more accurate). Being part of the out crowd makes you long for things to be different. And the only real hope for things to be different is for the world to change. It makes you long for the next stage.

The psalmist writes,

"Awake! Why are You sleeping, O Lord? Rouse Yourself! Do not reject us forever!" If I had been writing this psalm in my precollege years, I would have said, "Lord, when will the next stage come?"

Some Old Testament scholars think this psalm may have been written during the later stages of the Diaspora, when the nation of Judah was ruled by Babylon and all of the Israelites were living somewhere other than the promised land. That would have been a difficult time to be an Israelite, especially after hearing for generation after generation that God promises to save His people from their oppressor, yet here they were in Babylon and still under Babylonian rule.

I know there were times when I was growing up when God's promises rang hollow. I certainly wasn't getting any more popular. And despite my efforts to be kind to others, there didn't seem to be much reward in it. Yet, during some of those yearly activities—at summer camps and winter retreats—I would be removed from my regular world and I would catch a glimpse of God's promises. I would hear Him speaking. Those events showed me that other Christians were willing to be my friend. And even after I went home, I knew the community I longed for existed. It was enough to give me hope and keep me pushing ahead to the next stage.

Those next stages did come. And with each stage came an opportunity to meet new people, make new friends, and establish a different identity. And each new stage was better, but it eventually gave way to a new longing for the new next stage. The road from age 9 to age 18 seemed inordinately long, filled with what seemed like an endless longing for the next stage.

The psalmist's next stage did eventually come. If the scholars are right, it was under Greek rule. While the Israelites were able to return to their homeland, it wasn't long before they were longing again for their next stage, probably turning again to this lament.

Despite the eternal longing for the next stage I had as a child, my faith in God's promises never foundered. I know there were times I cried, times I was fed up, times I wished God would just take me to heaven already. But He didn't leave me. We kept moving forward to the next stage together.

"Redeem us for the sake of Your steadfast love!" (v. 26)

The most important thing that I knew about God when I was growing up was that He loves me. Contextually, that means everything. It means that if the world isn't working out the way I want or if I think my life doesn't mean much, God still loves me. Jesus still saves me. If I have any doubts, I need only to look at the cross. Jesus didn't die for nothing, He did it because God loves me. He did it because He loves you.

The psalmist obviously did not have the full perspective of knowing God's plan for salvation, but the love of God was not lost on the writer.

I have now spent almost as much time out of school as I did in. I'm a little less gangly than I was as child and, if I keep my mouth shut, you might not peg me as geeky. The talking too much part isn't much different, but I guess not everything changes. I stopped my constant longing for the next stage during college when I met the woman who is now my wife. God has given me many blessings since that time, including some really spectacular jobs, a daughter, and a lifelong friend to love (my wife). Sometimes I forget there is anything to long for.

Men, we are strangers in a strange land and earth is not our home. Next stages still come and go in our lives, but we still have one next stage that will be great. No more tears. No more mean people. No more failures. No more job searches. No more sin. Someday our relationships will be perfect and we won't cause anyone to be hurt or sad by our actions. We can wait for the heaven stage both patiently and longingly because God's love has redeemed us through our Savior, Jesus Christ.

> Men, we are strangers in a strange land and earth is not our home. Next stages still come and go in our lives, but we still have one next stage that will be great.
>
> *Prayer: Blessed Holy Spirit, keep my eyes fixed on Jesus, the author and perfecter of my faith, and help me to walk blamelessly in God's sight until the day I meet my Lord face-to-face. I ask this in His name. Amen.*

Friday

1. In what stage of life do you find yourself today? What's next for you?

2. In what sense is it right to long for what is next, and in what sense is such longing problematic?

3. The psalmist essentially urges God to wake up and take care of His people (v. 23). What does this way of talking say about his relationship with God?

4. Why are "dust" and "ground" (earth) such potent images of human sorrow and suffering?

5. In spite of the sad and even desperate tone of the psalm, where does the psalmist at last arrive when he reaches the final verse?

Week One

Psalm 44

The 44th psalm is a general psalm of prayer in which all the saints, especially the New Testament saints, lament that they are persecuted by the heathen and tyrants and would be slaughtered. They cry out that God has given them over to this, as if He had abandoned them. Formerly He had helped them with great wonders, and no harm came to them from persecutions. But they are now even persecuted on their own account, that is, for God's sake, as if they had done all kinds evil. In summary, this psalm is the sighing of the spirit. It rebukes the flesh, which murmurs against God that it is judged unrighteous and is so poorly governed (according to reason) that the godly, who ought to be helped, are allowed to suffer, and the evil, who ought to be punished, are elevated.

-Martin Luther

1. When do you feel the most secure and safe? What factors contribute significantly to this feeling? What things pose the greatest threat to that sense of well-being and security?

2. How is the conquest of Canaan (described in v. 2) a cause of hope and a source of comfort for the psalmist? How can remembering past blessings from God provide you with present comfort and security? What events from your past give you present hope?

3. How important is the Church's work of telling the story of God's love and actions for His people? How should the Church do this work?

4. People use many images to convey their understanding of God: grandfather, friend, counselor, hero, etc. How does the image of God as king (v. 4) change one's view of God? How might this image impact a person's view of his relationship with God?

5. What does it mean to spend a day boasting in God? How can we justify such boasting when God calls us to be humble and to reject all arrogance?

6. What does the image of a sheep cheaply sold for butchering (vv. 11–12) convey about the worth of a human being? Is there any sense in which this graphic and disquieting image is still applicable for Christians?

7. Can God's people expect any special treatment when it comes to the hassles and hurts that define life in this world? How is it possible that being one of God's people may actually invite *more* pain and sorrow?

8. What do you say to fellow Christians who do not understand how God can be so slow to answer their prayers or apparently unwilling to spare them from sorrow and pain in spite of their faithfulness?

9. Why do you think Psalm 44 (and others like it) with its dark tone and sometimes-pessimistic attitude is included in the Psalter? What benefit is there in studying this psalm?

10. What attitude or life changes does the message of this psalm demand of you? How will it affect the way that you face the week's challenges or the way that you work to encourage others?

Week Two

Psalm 74

[1] O God, why do You cast us off forever? Why does Your anger smoke against the sheep of Your pasture?

[2] Remember your congregation, which You have purchased of old, which You have redeemed to be the tribe of Your heritage! Remember Mount Zion, where You have dwelt.

[3] Direct Your steps to the perpetual ruins;
the enemy has destroyed everything in the sanctuary!

[4] Your foes have roared in the midst of Your meeting place; they set up their own signs for signs.

[5] They were like those who swing axes in a forest of trees.

[6] And all its carved wood they broke down with hatchets and hammers.

[7] They set Your sanctuary on fire; they profaned the dwelling place of Your name, bringing it down to the ground.

[8] They said to themselves, "We will utterly subdue them"; they burned all the meeting places of God in the land.

[9] We do not see our signs; there is no longer any prophet, and there is none among us who knows how long.

[10] How long, O God, is the foe to scoff?
Is the enemy to revile Your name forever?

[11] Why do You hold back Your hand, Your right hand?
Take it from the fold of Your garment and destroy them!

¹² Yet God my King is from of old,
working salvation in the midst of the earth.

¹³ You divided the sea by Your might;
You broke the heads of the sea monsters on the waters.

¹⁴ You crushed the heads of Leviathan;
You gave him as food for the creatures of the wilderness.

¹⁵ You split open springs and brooks;
You dried up ever-flowing streams.

¹⁶ Yours is the day, Yours also the night;
You have established the heavenly lights and the sun.

¹⁷ You have fixed all the boundaries of the earth;
You have made summer and winter.

¹⁸ Remember this, O LORD, how the enemy scoffs,
and a foolish people reviles Your name.

¹⁹ Do not deliver the soul of Your dove to the wild
beasts; do not forget the life of Your poor forever.

²⁰ Have regard for the covenant, for the dark places
of the land are full of the habitations of violence.

²¹ Let not the downtrodden turn back in shame;
let the poor and needy praise Your name.

²² Arise, O God, defend Your cause;
remember how the foolish scoff at You all the day!

²³ Do not forget the clamor of Your foes, the uproar of
those who rise against You, which goes up continually!

John Shimkus

Psalm 74:1–3

> O God, why do You cast us off forever? Why does Your anger smoke against the sheep of Your pasture? Remember Your congregation, which You have purchased of old, which You have redeemed to be the tribe of Your heritage! Remember Mount Zion, where You have dwelt. Direct Your steps to the perpetual ruins; the enemy has destroyed everything in the sanctuary!

Your Inner Politician

Please allow me to introduce myself. My name is John Shimkus. I am the husband of Karen and the father of three sons: David, Joshua, and Daniel. My family and I live in my hometown, Collinsville, Illinois, where we attend Holy Cross Lutheran Church. I also represent the Nineteenth Congressional District of Illinois in the U.S. House of Representatives.

As a politician, I often tease my constituents by saying, "You know, my profession is the most honest of them all." Always curious, sometimes confused, and occasionally rebuffing my attempt at humor, they frequently compel me to defend my claim. Like attorneys, politicians are acutely aware of the jokes about their profession, especially those having the words "honest" and "politician" in the same sentence.

Politicians have to make decisions just like other people. Sometimes those decisions are easy. Many times the decisions we are called upon to make are tough, especially when the stakes are high or when there is strong disagreement about an issue. Individuals and groups of people use different processes in making decisions; we can call them *decision matrixes*. These matrixes usually analyze both costs and benefits of any proposal, probing all the many variables that need to be considered.

One variable that is inevitably part of the decision matrix is the *political variable*. The wishes of the constituency, future offices one wishes to run for, congressional leadership positions, and so on must be considered. This is neither good nor bad;

it is just the reality of politics. If queried why a decision was made, politicians will frequently refer to the political variable as one of the many factors that influenced their decision.

Politicians are honest when they admit that the political variable is part of their decision matrix. But when they don't, their failure at transparency and honesty can cause confusion, mistrust, and anger.

The writer of Psalm 74, a member of the Asaph family, knew something about politics. Apparently the psalm was written after the city of Jerusalem and its temple were destroyed by the Babylonians in 587 BC. Imagine your capital city and center of worship lying in smoking ruins. Imagine further your own people being exiled to a foreign land. Few of us today have lived through such terrifying ordeals. But those who have, including veterans, survivors of 9/11, and those who've suffered at the hands of violent, cruel, and, yes, dishonest people know something about this. They are familiar with the feeling of abandonment, even abandonment by God. Like the psalmist, they have cried out, "Look at this, God! Don't You see what has happened? Don't You remember Your people, Your sanctuary? Look what Your enemies have done!"

That can happen in a congregation too. Verse 3 says, "The enemy has destroyed everything in the sanctuary." Because God has made us social creatures, we need politics, which is simply the process we use to make decisions. Our decision matrix. We need politics, even in the church. But our enemy—Satan—can twist our decision-making process in order to destroy the fellowship, mission, and unity of a church. Sometimes churches require the use of a "reconciler" to help restore unity. Sometimes the self-interests of individuals or groups within a congregation make up the political variable that everyone knows about but only a few are willing to admit. Only the Gospel preached and the Sacraments administered can help bring healing and hope in such situations.

When misused, church politics can limit the effectiveness of God's kingdom here on earth. Peter says that "the devil prowls around like a roaring lion, seeking someone to devour" (1 Peter 5:78). James asks, "What causes quarrels and what causes fights among you? Is it not this, that your passions are at war within you?" (James 4:1). Those involved in conflict should take into account their own conflicting feelings and passionate desires, which James says is the source of "quarrels" and "fights." By being honest with ourselves, and by promoting transparency and mutual confession, church leaders, professional church workers, and congregation members can learn to be more sympathetic to one another's faults, extend their forgiveness to those who have wronged them, and work toward building trust. Such an environment will aid in building God's kingdom through Christ's Word and Spirit.

Luther noted that Psalm 74 was a prayer against the enemies of the Church. And in truth, while we pray for the conversion of souls through the spiritual means of the Gospel and the Sacraments, we also pray that God would bring to justice those who perpetuate injustice against His people. But we pray this prayer with great humility, realizing that once we also were God's enemies, fully in league with Satan and aligned with sin and death. But God in His great mercy did not leave us in that awful state. Paul writes,

> God shows His love for us in that while we were still sinners, Christ died for us. Since, therefore, we have now been justified by His blood, much more shall we be saved by Him from the wrath of God. For if while we were enemies we were reconciled to God by the death of His Son, much more, now that we are reconciled, shall we be saved by His life. More than that, we also rejoice in God through our Lord Jesus Christ, through whom we have now received reconciliation. (Romans 5:8–11)

God reconciled us to Himself through the death and resurrection of His Son. Can He not through His Spirit reconcile us to one another? I believe that He can and that He does. Through the Law, God's Spirit confronts us with our sinful selves and with the times we've allowed our own internal war to bubble over into angry and self-serving words and deeds. But through the Gospel of God's reconciling love in Christ, that same Spirit renews our spirits with the hope and peace we have through Jesus Christ, our Lord.

So regardless of the decision you may have to make right now or sometime in the future, take into account your internal politician. Be honest with yourself, with your God, with your family and friends, and with your co-workers. In spite of the situation, however bad, God has not forgotten you. In Jesus, God has remembered His people and His sanctuary. Our enemy the devil is defeated, and you are reconciled to God through faith in Christ.

God reconciled us to Himself through the death and resurrection of His Son. Can He not through His Spirit reconcile us to one another? I believe that He can and that He does.

Prayer: Heavenly Father, help me to use the gifts of human reason and relationships according to Your will. Grant me a cooperative and selfless spirit, so that Your name might be glorified and Your people be blessed. In Jesus' name. Amen.

Monday

Psalm 74:1-3

1. What was a decision you made recently that was carefully calculated for a "political" advantage?

2. What are the main forces that propel your personal "decision matrix"?

3. In what sense are the psalmist's opening questions really about *God's* "decision matrix"?

4. Why is this opening prayer a remarkable declaration of faith in God?

5. What does this psalm teach you about your own "decision matrix" when the flow of life seems to be completely against you?

Psalm 74:4-7

Your foes have roared in the midst of Your meeting place;
they set up their own signs for signs. They were like those who
swing axes in a forest of trees. And all its carved wood they
broke down with hatchets and hammers. They set Your sanctuary on fire; they profaned the dwelling place of Your name,
bringing it down to the ground.

A Name Above

A colleague and I were spending long hours in a committee markup of a bill. Essentially, committee markup is the process of putting a bill into its final form, normally through amendment, before it is brought to the House floor for a vote. To break the tension during this process, my colleague shared with me an address book of the Members of Congress who served in 1937.

At that time, there were twenty-five members of the House of Representatives representing the State of Illinois. (Today, there are only nineteen.) As members of the Seventy-fifth Congress of the United States, those Illinois congressmen were part of establishing the National Cancer Institute, criminalizing marijuana, and extending existing neutrality laws, which helped to keep the United States out of war until 1941.

My friend's small booklet had all the House members' names and the addresses of their homes in Washington, D.C. As I was paging through the booklet, Ed asked me if I recognized any names. At that time I replied that, while I was familiar with some of the towns and communities, I was less familiar with most of the names. I went on to say, "That that will be us someday: 'big shots' today who are easily forgotten tomorrow."

The psalm writer continues his lament following the destruction of Jerusalem and its temple. The glory days of Judah were gone, and it was difficult to reconcile the love that God had shown His covenant people in the past with the devastation that now surrounded them. The Babylonian hordes had breached Jerusalem's walls and had violated their holy places. Most notably, they had profaned the most holy place on earth, God's dwelling place, the place where He placed His name.

The psalm writer describes in vivid detail how Babylonian soldiers "roared in the midst of [God's] meeting place," and "were like those who swing axes in a forest of trees. . . all its carved wood they broke down with hatchets and hammers" (vv. 4–6). Recall the grandeur and splendor of Solomon's magnificent temple. Its inner walls were paneled with cedar and its floors with pine; the wooden walls were carved with gourds, flowers, palm trees, and cherubim. The Most Holy Place, the small room containing the ark of the covenant, glistened with gold: the ceiling, the walls, and the floors.

Now imagine golden splinters flying midair as the Babylonian infidels swung and chopped and hammered the interior of the temple to pieces. The destruction was devastating.

For America, the bombing of Pearl Harbor on December 7, 1941, was devastating. With 2,403 dead, including 1,177 from the USS Arizona alone, the United States was compelled to dispense with neutrality and finally enter World War II. It would be the Seventy-seventh Congress that Franklin Delano Roosevelt would call upon to deal with this attack and to formally declare war on Japan the next day.

Verses 5–6 highlight the transitory nature of this present life that leaves only devastation in its path. The plans we make, the buildings we construct, the ships we build, the military might we amass, the wealth we create, the alliances we form, even our earthly bodies are here today and gone tomorrow. In another psalm, King David wrote,

> O LORD, make me know my end and what is the measure
> of my days; let me know how fleeting I am! Behold, You have
> made my days a few handbreadths, and my lifetime is as noth-
> ing before You. Surely all mankind stands as a mere breath!
> *Selah.* (Psalm 39:4–5)

Even the name we try to make for ourselves now will someday be forgotten. True, our names may be recorded in a newspaper, a history book, the family Bible, or even in the Congressional Record, but someday it will be forgotten by most people.

Not so the name of the Lord (Yahweh). You know, there is a special significance for the Lord placing His name upon His dwelling place. In Old Testament times, this was the temple. Where God placed His name, there He was. But not in the usual way that we think of Him being, that is, being everywhere at the same time. No, where God places His name He is present in a special, gracious, sin-forgiving way. The Lord Himself instituted the special sacrifices of the temple, the place of His name, which all pointed forward to the sacrifice that Jesus would make for us on the cross (see Hebrews 9–10).

Jesus (whose name means "Yahweh saves") is the fulfillment of the Old Testament temple. Jesus stated so in John 2:19: "Destroy this temple, and in three days I will raise it up." Jesus used the special word for the Most Holy Place, the place of God's gracious presence on earth. John explains in verse 21, "But [Jesus] was speaking about the temple of His body." Jesus was and is God's true Most Holy Place, the person to whom we can come with our hopes, our dreams, our frustrations, and yes, our sins. Jesus, God in human flesh, was crucified and resurrected for us. Jesus saves!

Time is fleeting. Our life work, our reputations, and eventually our names and reputations will pass away in this life. So if we are to labor, we should labor for the Lord. We should work for things above. Jesus said,

> Do not lay up for yourselves treasures on earth, where moth and rust destroy and where thieves break in and steal, but lay up for yourselves treasures in heaven, where neither moth nor rust destroys and where thieves do not break in and steal. (Matthew 6:19–20)

Jesus also said, "Seek first the kingdom of God and His righteousness, and all these things will be added to you" (Matthew 6:33). In this way, you will store up what truly matters in heaven. What you build there through faith here will never be broken down or destroyed. And there no one will forget your name, for it has been written in the Lamb's Book of Life.

....

Our life work, our reputations, and eventually our names and reputations will pass away in this life. So if we are to labor, we should labor for the Lord.

Prayer: Lord Jesus Christ, Your name is above all names. Thank You for saving me by Your grace. Help me to honor Your name with pure speech and a chaste life, so that others might praise You forever and ever. In Your name I pray. Amen.

....

Tuesday

1. What times, places, or circumstances have a way of making you feel small and insignificant?

2. What vivid scene is being described in verses 4-7? What gives it the sense of immediacy that would come with a firsthand account?

3. How does the sad fate of Solomon's temple and the city of Jerusalem serve as a stern warning also to you today?

4. In the world of tolerance and understanding in which we purportedly live, is the kind of hatred evidenced in these verses still a reality for you? What reasons do you have for your answer?

5. What's the best way to react when an ax-wielding maniac is trying to destroy the things of God—including the child of God—you?

Psalm 74:8–11

They said to themselves, "We will utterly subdue them";
they burned all the meeting places of God in the land. We do
not see our signs; there is no longer any prophet, and there is
none among us who knows how long. How long, O God, is the
foe to scoff? Is the enemy to revile Your name forever? Why
do You hold back Your hand, Your right hand? Take it from the
fold of Your garment and destroy them!

God's Saving Name

I often joke that in Washington, D.C. a member of Congress will be thought of as an expert in an area of the world due to the ethnicity of his or her last name. This has happened to me.

My family name is Shimkus, which is of Lithuanian ancestry. However, like many Americans, I am a "Heinz 57"—an all-American mutt. I am also a mixture of German, Irish, and some believe, American Indian ancestry. But my family name (some believe Shimkus means "Simon," others say it means "raft-man") has given me the opportunity to learn about, support, and come to love the small, beautiful, and courageous country of Lithuania.

Because the heritage of my family name is Lithuanian, I have been "adopted" by the Lithuanian-American community in the United States. Although I live in Collinsville, Illinois, as a congressman I spend much time in Washington, D.C. on congressional business. One additional duty that has turned into a labor of love is promoting and advocating for the Baltic countries of Lithuania, Latvia, and Estonia.

Vilnius, the capitol of Lithuania, was considered "the Jerusalem of Lithuania" prior to World War II. Before the war, there were more than ten synagogues and at least ten yeshivas, or Jewish schools, in the city. Like in many cities in Europe, the Jewish community in Vilnius was ravaged by the Holocaust. Before Nazi atrocities, 30 percent of the city of Vilnius was Jewish. Today, that number is only .5 percent.

Psalm 74:8 says, "They said to themselves, 'We will utterly subdue them'; they burned all the meeting places of God in the land." In the King James Version of the Bible, "meeting places" is translated as "synagogues," so this passage would sound hauntingly familiar to Jews still living in Vilnius today. Because this psalm was written during the reign of King David, it is a prophecy about the destruction of synagogues that had yet to be built. The Babylonians would come and destroy the temple in Jerusalem and the places where God's Word was taught in Judah. And 3,000 years later, in Vilnius and in other places in Europe, the Nazis would show their same hatred for God's Word as the Babylonians had done in Judah.

The persecution of any ethnic or religious minority, especially the Jewish people, is a sad blight on the human race. While there are examples of Christians making sacrifices for the persecuted, even in World War II, too often our story is one of failing to stand up for, love, and sacrifice for our neighbor who needs it the most. In the Old Testament, God is frequently referred to as the God of the orphan and the widow—those who the weakest in society. Various Hebrew laws protected the rights of the poor and the respect for the foreigner. God still considers gracious hospitality and a concern for the well-being of those who are less fortunate as virtues. He also considers justice for the weak and defenseless as an important goal for His people.

Who among the weak, who among us, has not felt like the psalmist crying out to God, "How long, O God, is the foe to scoff? Is the enemy to revile Your name forever?" (v. 10). It would seem that almighty God, who made everything that exists, the "visible and invisible" as we say in the Nicene Creed, would not take it too lightly that His name was being misused. But this verse means much more than that. It is not just that the psalmist laments evildoers being disrespectful with God's name; no, they also show disrespect toward God specifically in how they treat His children. Think about that. We are not only to love God with all our hearts, souls, and minds but we are also to love our neighbors as ourselves (Luke 10:27). John wrote, "Whoever says he is in the light and hates his brother is still in darkness. Whoever loves his brother abides in the light, and in him there is no cause for stumbling" (1 John 2:9–10). The love of God and the love of neighbor are inseparable.

How that stands in contrast to some views of some people and politicians in the world! Adherents to radical Islam consider it a duty to attack Jewish people. The elected president of a foreign country promotes wiping the State of Israel off of the face of the earth. How hatred of one's neighbor is so intimately connected with hatred of God's name! Yet the inverse is also true: true love of God and His name is connected with true love of neighbor. Listen to the apostle Paul:

> Have this mind among yourselves, which is yours in Christ Jesus, who, though He was in the form of God, did not count equality with God a thing to be grasped, but made Himself

nothing, taking the form of a servant, being born in the likeness of men. And being found in human form, He humbled Himself by becoming obedient to the point of death, even death on a cross. (Philippians 2:5–8)

Jesus was and is God's love in action, having perfect obedience to His Father's will and a love so deep that He went all the way to the cross. Not just for certain people, but for all people, for you and for me. And because Jesus honored His Father's name by His obedience and His love,

God has highly exalted Him and bestowed on Him the name that is above every name, so that at the name of Jesus every knee should bow, in heaven and on earth and under the earth, and every tongue confess that Jesus Christ is Lord, to the glory of God the Father. (vv. 9–11)

Jesus says, "Love your enemies, do good to those who hate you, bless those who curse you, pray for those who abuse you" (Luke 6:27–28). Men, you already bear the name "Christian." What can you do to testify to the saving name of Jesus? What can you do to defend the weak and powerless, the child needing adoption, the unborn? You may be called upon to stand your ground for your faith, and you may be called even further to pay a tremendous penalty for it. But God in His grace will give you the strength.

Through faith in Christ, you already kneel at the name of Jesus, your Savior and Lord. Be courageous and stand firm in His saving name, for on the Last Day even His enemies will kneel.

. . . .

Jesus was and is God's love in action, having perfect obedience to His Father's will and a love so deep that He went all the way to the cross.

Prayer: Dear Lord, sometimes I do not wish to attend services in Your house. Through Your Word, transform me to be like Your Son, so that as Your servant, I might bring glory to Your name. I ask this for the sake of Christ, my Lord. Amen.

. . . .

Wednesday

Psalm 74:8–11

1. Why does coming to the side of the weak and powerless pose a greater risk than helping the powerful and influential?

2. What does God stand to gain from His intervention on behalf of the weak and the powerless?

3. What is the connection between God's slowness to act on behalf of His people and the character or worthiness of those people?

4. What do these verses teach about the way to respond when God is silent?

5. Given the message of these verses, how do you need to adjust your attitude toward the chronic challenges that seem impervious to both your efforts and your prayers?

Psalm 74:12-17

Yet God my King is from of old, working salvation in the midst of the earth. You divided the sea by Your might; You broke the heads of the sea monsters on the waters. You crushed the heads of Leviathan; You gave him as food for the creatures of the wilderness. You split open springs and brooks; You dried up ever-flowing streams. Yours is the day, Yours also the night; You have established the heavenly lights and the sun. You have fixed all the boundaries of the earth; You have made summer and winter.

Be Not Ashamed

Even though I work in national government, I do not spend much time watching the various political pundits on TV, cable, or the Internet. These pundits are watching me and my colleagues, waiting for every opportunity to exploit our weaknesses or highlight our mistakes. Many of us are used as convenient fodder for their audiences. This too has happened to me.

We have had many hearings about global warming on the Hill. One particular day, a member of clergy and another faith-based organization testified before us. Because there is much concern about the arctic ice melting and a subsequent rise in sea levels, I thought I would put man's analysis side-by-side with God's Word. It seemed to fit, since those testifying represented faith communities. I quoted Genesis 9:15, which states God's promise never to destroy again the earth by a flood:

I will remember My covenant that is between Me and you and every living creature of all flesh. And the waters shall never again become a flood to destroy all flesh.

After my comment, I was attacked for expressing my faith. In a follow-up profile, a reporter stated that I had marginalized myself by my comments. She went on to question my assertion that the earth would never again be destroyed by a flood and that the seasons of the years would remain. I responded, "Yes, that is what I believe." I believe all of God's Word.

But with the reporter's question came the opportunity to bear witness to my faith and to the truthfulness of Scripture. I asked her, "If you question the accounts of the flood, the promises of God, the parting of the Red Sea and by that the destruction of Pharaoh's army, why not question the divinity, sacrifice, and resurrection of Christ?" Based on what eventually became her story, I believe the reporter thought that I was being sincere, although she never quoted my profession of faith.

Psalm 74:13 says, "You divided the sea by Your might; You broke the heads of the sea monsters on the waters." In this passage, the psalmist is talking about God exercising His mighty power over the forces of the deep. All of creation—including its mysterious watery depths—was created by His fatherly hand and is under His constant control. A frightening thought to be sure—God's limitless power manifest in the forces of nature—but a comforting thought once we consider God's compassion and grace in Jesus Christ. God's power is not only over us but it is also for us. That's why the psalmist notes in verse 12, "God my King is from of old, working salvation in the midst of the earth."

That's what we see in these verses: God's power in and through water on behalf of His people, specifically in His parting of the Red Sea. Here we could ask, Did God really divide the Red Sea to allow the children of Israel to escape Pharaoh? Did God really call the water to return, thus crushing Pharaoh's mighty army? Did God really save His people through these waters? I believe the answer is Yes, and it is important to affirm that belief. Why? Because in the end, to question God's ability to perform miracles on behalf of His people is also to question His ability to save.

Human nature wants to believe what it can wrap its mind around; the part of Scripture that seems unreasonable or conflicts with our worldview or agenda, or calls into question our motives or "beliefs" or behaviors, is ruled out-of-bounds. But when we believe only those parts of God's Word we want to believe, that calls our whole belief system into question, doesn't it? After all, do we really think we sinful human beings are able to determine which verses in Scripture are true and which are false? That puts our faith not in God but in human nature.

Paul writes, "For I am not ashamed of the gospel, for it is the power of God for salvation to everyone who believes, to the Jew first and also to the Greek" (Romans 1:16). The Gospel is God's powerful love for us in Christ Jesus, who atoned for our sins on the cross and rose again on the third day for our justification. His great love for me liberates me from thinking I can separate truth from fiction, fact from fable, in His Word. In fact, His great love for me enables me to embrace Him as my God and Savior and embrace His Word as holy and without error, just as He is holy and without error.

Those who discredit the truthfulness of God's promises in Scripture, or reject the historicity of events such as the Red Sea crossing, really need to take Jesus seriously. It's logically inconsistent to believe that Jesus tells us the truth when He speaks about our salvation but that He was mistaken when He spoke about passages from the Old Testament. In the Gospel of Matthew, Jesus frequently quotes Old Testament prophecies and affirms that they were coming to pass in Him. Because Jesus believed and taught that all of God's Word is reliable, you and I can do the same.

I am neither ashamed of the Gospel of Christ, nor am I ashamed of the powerful works of God shown to man throughout human history and recorded in His Word. The psalmist writes, "Yours is the day, Yours also the night; You have established the heavenly lights and the sun. You have fixed all the boundaries of the earth; You have made summer and winter" (vv. 16–17). Knowing that our gracious, Creator God is in control of all things, that He always tells us the truth, and that He loves us gives you and me the confidence we need when we confess our faith.

Be encouraged and, as Paul wrote to Timothy, "Fight the good fight of the faith. Take hold of the eternal life to which you were called and about which you made the good confession in the presence of many witnesses" (1 Timothy 6:12).

....

Jesus frequently quotes Old Testament prophecies and affirms that they were coming to pass in Him. Because Jesus believed and taught that all of God's Word is reliable, you and I can do the same.

Prayer: Heavenly Father, grant me the faith to believe in Your Word and to accept even those things that I do not understand. You have proven Yourself faithful and trustworthy in all things, for which I give You thanks and praise. In Jesus' name. Amen.

....

Thursday

Daily Study Questions
Psalm 74:12–17

1. When are the times that you are most tempted not to speak out about your faith?

2. The devotion operates with an important distinction: do you trust the Bible because you trust Jesus, or do you trust Jesus because you trust the Bible?

3. What provides the foundation for the psalmist's unwavering trust in his God?

4. Why is it significant that this powerful God is also the author and master of night (verse 16) and winter (verse 17)?

5. How does this description of God's might over the created realm reassure you as you face twenty-first-century monsters?

Psalm 74:18-23

Remember this, O LORD, how the enemy scoffs, and a foolish people reviles Your name. Do not deliver the soul of Your dove to the wild beasts; do not forget the life of Your poor forever. Have regard for the covenant, for the dark places of the land are full of the habitations of violence. Let not the downtrodden turn back in shame; let the poor and needy praise Your name. Arise, O God, defend Your cause; remember how the foolish scoff at You all the day! Do not forget the clamor of Your foes, the uproar of those who rise against You, which goes up continually!

The Unforgivable Sin

For years now, I have taught an adult Bible study class at Holy Cross Lutheran Church in Collinsville, Illinois. It has been a great experience for me, as it forces me into God's Word and allows me the opportunity to profess my faith and the doctrine of our church.

As it happens, many times our talks in Bible class have led us to a discussion of the "unforgivable sin" described in Mark 3:29 (the ESV calls it "an eternal sin"). This verse is difficult for many people because it seems to conflict with other passages of the Bible. How can a God who loves us and sent His Son to die for us not forgive a certain sin? Didn't Jesus die for all sins? Aren't all sins forgiven through faith in Him?

The "unforgivable sin" is even more challenging when we admit that we are all sinful. Born with original sin, the sin we inherited from Adam, we are all under God's condemnation. We're born with three strikes against us. In fact, Psalm 51:5 says, "I was brought forth in iniquity, and in sin did my mother conceive me." So, we're sinful even from the very moment of our conception. So as to leave no doubt, after we are born our own actions condemn us. So with all this sin, and God in Christ forgiving all of it, how can there be one sin that isn't forgiven?

Here, I believe, Psalm 74 can help.

Luther saw Psalm 74 as a prayer against God's enemies, those who destroyed Jerusalem, its temple, and the land. In its original context, it served as a prayer against the Babylonians. But for Christians, Luther also interpreted this psalm as a prayer against those who would seek to destroy God's Word and Christ's Church. Verse 18 says, "Remember this, O LORD, how the enemy scoffs, and a foolish people reviles Your name." Remember how Jesus instructed His disciples to "hallow" God's name? In contrast, God's enemies, the scoffers and the foolish people, are those who reject Christ, those who have heard God's message of reconciliation in the Messiah and have turned against it.

The unforgivable sin is "unyielding refusal to believe the Gospel and a rejection of the Holy Spirit's work to create faith in Jesus" (*The Lutheran Study Bible*, p. 1661). To reject God and His promises in Christ is blasphemy against the Holy Spirit. Sometimes those who have rejected God's mercy in Christ go so far as to seek to destroy God's Word and His people; that's what this psalm is about—it is a prayer for God to defend Israel (Luther would include the new Israel) against her enemies. In the same way that ancient Israel's enemies sought to destroy her, so too do the enemies of Christ's Church rail against her. But Jesus Himself promises that she will prevail (Matthew 16:18).

Paul writes, "We implore you on behalf of Christ, be reconciled to God." (2 Corinthians 5:20). God's message to the world is this: Be reconciled to Me! Elsewhere, Paul writes, "If you confess with your mouth that Jesus is Lord and believe in your heart that God raised Him from the dead, you will be saved" (Romans 10:9). The promise of salvation is for *all* people, including scoffers and revilers. As John 3:16 makes clear, out of His great love for all people God sent Jesus into the world to suffer and die for all sins. That includes the unforgivable sin. In and of itself that *sin* is not unforgiven, because God forgave all sins in Christ through His death on the cross. It's just that the *person* who persistently rejects God's forgiveness in Christ remains unforgiven.

However, Psalm 74 shows Asaph to be a man of faith. Asaph prays to God, asking Him to deliver His people from their enemies and to "have regard for the covenant, for the dark places of the land are full of the habitations of violence" (v. 20). The covenant is God's promise of salvation through His Messiah, the unconditional covenant of grace God established with Abraham and His descendents forever (see Genesis 15). God's Old Testament believers were saved through faith in the coming Messiah. You and I are Abraham's descendents and recipients of that covenant through faith in Christ (Galatians 3:7–9). Jesus is Abraham's promised "offspring" (v. 16); through Him, God's covenant has come into effect. We likewise are saved through faith in Him.

God knows that as long as they live in this sin-ravaged world, His faithful people dwell in the land of violence. They will be oppressed by His enemies. Therefore, the psalmist calls upon the Lord to remember the gracious, covenantal promises He made to His people and to rescue them. Or as Jesus taught us to pray, "Deliver us from evil." Before Christ came into our lives, we also were "downtrodden" by sin, Satan, and death. We were spiritually "poor and needy" (Psalm 74:21). Because we have been reconciled to God through Christ, however, we are able to "praise [His] name." Even more, the same Spirit who brought us to faith in our Savior enables us to have compassion for those who have not yet heard God's message of reconciliation. The Spirit moves us also to proclaim, "Be reconciled to God!"

Confident of God's mercy in Christ, with Asaph we can pray, "Arise, O God, defend Your cause" (v. 22). The scoffers are unceasing in their scoffing, and God's foes are unrelenting in insulting His name and the name of His people. But God will prevail. Asaph's prayer is more than just a prayer for the Lord to defend His reputation among hardened unbelievers, or even our reputation as His people. It is a prayer also for the Lord to defend all the downtrodden, all the poor and needy—His human children who need to hear the message of the cross (1 Corinthians 1:18).

May God grant us the strength and courage to fight valiantly in His spiritual battle, confident that we are reconciled to Him through faith in Christ, certain of the power of the Gospel of Christ, and assured that the victory is already His through His Son.

....

The same Spirit who brought us to faith in our Savior enables us to have compassion for those who have not yet heard God's message of reconciliation. The Spirit moves us also to proclaim, "Be reconciled to God!"

Prayer: Holy Father, You reconciled the whole world to Yourself through Christ's sacrifice on the cross. Stir up within me a great love for all people, and grant me opportunities to tell others about what You have done through Christ, My Lord. In His name I pray. Amen.

....

Friday

1. Does your world fit the description of a "sin-ravaged land of violence"? Regardless your experience, what are some of the dark places in our land where violence dwells?

2. As he begins his final series of petitions, what is the psalmist's first concern? How should this example impact your own prayer life?

3. Why does the psalmist use the covenant in his effort to enlist God's intervening help? What promises might you similarly use?

4. What does it mean to let God plead His own cause (v. 22)? Why is this always a good idea?

5. Using this psalm as a model, what changes will you today implement in your own prayer life?

Week Two

Psalm 74

The 74th psalm is a psalm of prayer against the enemies who had laid waste Jerusalem, the temple, and all the schools of God in the land, together with the cities. Moreover, they slandered God, saying He could not help His people. However, the psalm appears as if it were a prayer against the destruction still to come, that is, of the Babylonians and thereafter by Antiochus Epiphanes. For only in these two instances was the temple in Jerusalem and the land destroyed. Accordingly, we pray this psalm against those who devastate Christendom, tear up God's Word, Sacraments, and all of God's ordinances, and thus clearly preach abomination and slander, and who continue everywhere.

-Martin Luther

1. What is the worst destruction you have personally experienced or witnessed?

2. The psalmist specifically mentions "Mount Zion" and "the sanctuary" as scenes of damage and ruin. Why are these places so significant? What message would this have sent to the people?

3. In the opening verses, the psalmist makes rather modest requests of God. For what does he hope and pray? Why might he be content to ask simply for this?

4. The psalm offers a striking and chilling picture of the temple's desecration and destruction—a frontal assault of Satan against the kingdom of God (vv. 4–7). What are some of the ways that Satan attacks God's Church in the twenty-first century? Are such frontal assaults a thing of the past?

5. In verse 4, the psalmist mentions one desecration in particular: the fact that the Babylonian invaders had actually placed their banners of war and conquest, their military standards, in the sanctuary of the temple. What are some ways that the world's "standards" have been set up in God's sanctuary, and the roar of the heathen heard in God's courts?

6. The destruction of the temple was tragic, but it did not exhaust the problems besetting the psalmist. According to verse 9, what further difficulty compounded Israel's woes? Do Christians today experience this sort of problem?

7. What is the name that is being reviled and spurned, seemingly forever, by the enemies of God? How does the confident declaration of Philippians 2:9–11 provide another perspective on this name and the duration of man's scorn of that name?

8. How does the dramatic shift in subject and tone from verse 12 through verse 17 change the lament and prayers that precede and follow these verses? Why do these verses have such a focused interest on God's rule over water and its creatures?

9. Which enemies, do you think, present the greatest threat to God's Church and its people? The psalmist, as usual, insists that such enemies are "foolish"—a word in Hebrew that means moral as well as intellectual deprivation. Is this still true in today's world? Why might many find it difficult to call such enemies "fools"?

10. Why do you think the psalmist gives special attention to those who are "downtrodden . . . poor and needy"? Who are the downtrodden, poor, and needy today? How does the Church fulfill this concern?

Week Three

Psalm 77

[1] I cry aloud to God, aloud to God, and He will hear me.

[2] In the day of my trouble I seek the Lord;
in the night my hand is stretched out without wearying;
my soul refuses to be comforted.

[3] When I remember God, I moan;
when I meditate, my spirit faints. *Selah*

[4] You hold my eyelids open;
I am so troubled that I cannot speak.

[5] I consider the days of old, the years long ago.

[6] I said, "Let me remember my song in the night; let me meditate in my heart." Then my spirit made a diligent search:

[7] "Will the Lord spurn forever, and never again be favorable?

[8] Has His steadfast love forever ceased?
Are His promises at an end for all time?

[9] Has God forgotten to be gracious?
Has He in anger shut up His compassion?" *Selah*

[10] Then I said, "I will appeal to this,
to the years of the right hand of the Most High."

[11] I will remember the deeds of the Lord;
yes, I will remember Your wonders of old.

¹² I will ponder all Your work,
and meditate on Your mighty deeds.

¹³ Your way, O God, is holy. What god is great like our God?

¹⁴ You are the God who works wonders;
You have made known Your might among the peoples.

¹⁵ You with Your arm redeemed your people,
the children of Jacob and Joseph. *Selah*

¹⁶ When the waters saw You, O God, when the waters
saw You, they were afraid; indeed, the deep trembled.

¹⁷ The clouds poured out water; the skies gave forth
thunder; Your arrows flashed on every side.

¹⁸ The crash of Your thunder was in the whirlwind; your light-
nings lighted up the world; the earth trembled and shook.

¹⁹ Your way was through the sea, Your path through
the great waters; yet Your footprints were unseen.

²⁰ You led Your people like a flock
by the hand of Moses and Aaron.

Steve Sandfort

Psalm 77:1–3

> I cry aloud to God, aloud to God, and He will hear me. In the day of my trouble I seek the Lord; in the night my hand is stretched out without wearying; my soul refuses to be comforted. When I remember God, I moan; when I meditate, my spirit faints. *Selah*

Days of Trouble

The day of my trouble began with a kiss goodbye to my wife, who was off to work and then to her parents' for the weekend. She had our only vehicle, so I was content to pedal around town on my new mountain bike, running errands for an upcoming youth retreat. However, ten minutes into my first errand, I noticed my wallet had fallen out of my pocket. I searched for it, but when it was clear I was not going to find it, I called the local police precinct and asked what my options were. I was told to come to the station and file a report.

I waited in line at the police department for more than an hour. I was losing my patience when the detective finally came out to greet me. He stayed only long enough to tell me that he could not file a report for a lost wallet, only for a stolen wallet. I couldn't convince him that someone must have stolen it after I lost it; that's why I couldn't find it when I went looking for it.

I was angry, especially with myself for getting into this mess. I sped my bike down Madison Street, not really watching what was ahead. Road construction had been ongoing, but that fact didn't hit me until I felt the thump of an orange cone against my shin. Immediately, I had that sinking feeling one gets when he has just ridden his new mountain bike into 8 inches of fresh concrete. "You all right?" the worker asked as he helped pull my bike out of the fresh road. The tires made a sucking sound, the sound that tires make when they are dislodged from wet concrete; it was a sound unlike anything I've heard before or since.

Now, don't feel bad for me yet. My day was only half over. After spending the afternoon chipping concrete off my new bike, the phone rang with the only good news I received all day. A man had found my wallet. He was willing to hold it for me until I could come to get it. I resisted the temptation to get back on the bike. Thankfully, my sister was in town that evening and she agreed to give me a ride. But first, one more errand; I needed to let the dog out for a family for whom my wife babysat. We drove to their beautiful house located in an exclusive neighborhood, and I proceeded to unlock the door. "Do they have an alarm?" my sister asked. "Yeah, but I know the code," I said.

Either the beeping alarm or the dog's barking made me stumble through the code the first try. When I finished my second attempt at the code, the alarm was still beeping, so I typed it in again. In the middle of my fourth attempt the house started making odd sounds. Lights flashed, horns blared, and even the dog shifted barking gears.

When the police showed up, things got a little dicey. The neighbors didn't recognize me or my sister. They were highly suspicious because my sister's car had out-of-state plates, and she is about a foot and a half shorter than me and bears almost no resemblance to me. The conversation went something like this: Police: "So, this is your sister?" Me: "Yes, sir!" Police: "Right . . . " (chuckle under breath).

For my part, I couldn't remember the name of the dog or all of the first names of the family who lived there. Things took a turn for the worst when they asked to see my I.D. (Refer to paragraphs 1 and 2.) So I stood against the police car with my hands outstretched while they called in my sister's I.D.

About the time they got back to me, the neighbor had gotten in touch with the family who lived in the house. They gave a good description to the police and everyone felt sure that I was legitimately who I said I was. And I did get my wallet back that night.

Reflect for a moment on a day when your life seemed to be coming apart at the seams. In Psalm 77, Asaph says, "In the day of my trouble I seek the Lord." Though that sounds pretty simple, in our day of trouble it's hard to stop and seek the Lord. We usually just get busy trying to fix the trouble. But God calls us to a different response; He calls us to seek Him.

When I'm seeking the Lord, I begin each task in prayer. I'm patient and humble. Unlike the day I just described, my actions are constructive and I am slow to anger. One would suppose everything would be superb if we would just seek the Lord, right? But in this psalm, it seems that even though Asaph is seeking the Lord, things are not getting better. Asaph says, "My soul refuses to be comforted." He was being tormented in his day of trouble and nothing could comfort him. He is describing a downward spiral that many of us have experienced. By verse 4, he has become so troubled that even prayer has become impossible.

Men, what Asaph needed was some good news. There is little else that can bring true comfort like good news. When I received the call that my wallet was found, I let out a huge sigh of relief. I was comforted. I forgot how angry I had been at the police department and how embarrassed I was as I pulled my bike out of the concrete. Good news brings relief. I was relieved after hearing the good news that I was not going to be booked for attempted burglary. Good news changes our whole outlook on life. That's why the Gospel is called the Good News. There is no better news than that which Jesus gives through the cross. You are forgiven and relieved of the burden of sin. Your day of trouble is over.

Let the Good News dwell in you richly this week. When your day of trouble approaches, seek the Lord and find everlasting comfort at the foot of His cross. Then go about your tasks filled with the knowledge that He will sustain you through all of your days, even your days of trouble. Amen!

....

Good news brings relief. . . . Good news changes our whole outlook on life. That's why the Gospel is called the Good News.

Prayer: Heavenly Father, when I have days filled with trouble, keep me humble. Grant me the grace to come to You in prayer, and sustain me with the Good News of my Savior, Jesus Christ. In His name I pray. Amen.

....

1. When you endured your last "day of trouble," were the problems of your own making, or were you simply the innocent victim of circumstances totally beyond your control?

2. Is it easy or difficult to turn to God when a day degenerates into a messy "day of trouble"? What does the source of your trouble have to do with where you look for the answer?

3. The psalmist does the right thing by turning to God when things get tough. What kind of response does he get from God? Why might this be?

4. The psalmist "refuses to be comforted" (v. 2); in other words, nothing helped his sorrow. Why might someone actually refuse comfort that is offered?

5. What can you do today to help you keep your focus on God, even when His answers are not immediately forthcoming?

Psalm 77:4-6

> You hold my eyelids open; I am so troubled that I cannot speak. I consider the days of old, the years long ago. I said, "Let me remember my song in the night; let me meditate in my heart." Then my spirit made a diligent search:

Remember Your Song

Before enrolling in seminary, I did some traveling and singing as a Christian recording artist. Writing, recording, and selling my own music were important parts of my life for almost fifteen years. The process of moving a song out of my heart and onto a piece of round plastic was one I enjoyed immensely. After writing a song, I would record the vocals and a basic guitar accompaniment. Then the producer would bring in session players to record the rest of the track. Sometimes chords were changed and melodies, tempos, and keys were manipulated along the way. Occasionally, when I went back into the booth to sing the final vocals, the song sounded quite a bit different from the original recording. In these cases, I struggled to learn the new versions of the songs. However, since I only had to get it right once, it eventually worked and the song was complete. Cassettes and CDs were manufactured, and I would sell them as I toured the country sharing the songs in churches, schools, coffeehouses, and camps.

Just after releasing my second album, I was on a promotional tour with five guys I loosely called my band. Our first concert was to be part of a special event in Milwaukee, before an expected crowd of thousands, far more people than I was used to playing for. I was excited, but I was also having difficulty getting the original versions of the songs out of my head. The band practiced as often as possible; however, most of the guys were also on the road with other artists quite often, so our time together in Nashville was limited.

I arrived in Milwaukee ahead of the band for some promotional events. For three days I did radio interviews, visited schools, and promoted the new CD in Christian bookstores. Everywhere I went, they wanted a little sample of the new CD. This was problematic because, without the band backing me, I only knew the songs the original way, playing my guitar as accompaniment. In three days, I must have played six events using the old versions of songs. When the band arrived in Milwaukee, we had a quick rehearsal and it became clear that I was going to have trouble. Nearly every song had some area where I was still singing or playing the old version. We had to end the rehearsal without truly ironing out the songs.

A few minutes before going on stage, we met for prayer. My prayer was almost identical to Asaph's words in Psalm 77:6. I prayed, "Lord, let me remember these songs tonight." It seems strange for me to pray that I could remember my own songs, but that's what my prayer was. How could something so close to me, that came out of my own heart, seem so far away now?

At times, even faith can seem hard to remember. Perhaps that is what Asaph was faced with. He longed for the memory of that song of faith within himself, the song that God had planted within him. That song would surely remind him of the steadfast love of God the Father. That song would bring peace to his troubled heart. But for Asaph, it was nowhere to be found. That song in his heart was lost.

Have you ever lost a child in a department store? Recently, I witnessed panic in the eyes and voice of a mother whose two boys had wandered off. She was optimistic that they were just goofing around in the men's restroom, but when I informed her they were not there, her expression turned from optimistic to troubled panic. There's a real urgency when someone or something we love is missing. Asaph shows this urgency, almost to the point of panic. When we read Psalm 77 in its entirety, we can almost hear the panic-stricken voice of Asaph.

So what are we to make of Asaph's troubled heart and the song he longs to remember? When I trace back over my life, the times I have been troubled have often been on account of my own turning away from God. This is certainly not always the case, but often when we are troubled because of our sin, God's Law is doing its job. Still, sometimes trouble comes to us by no fault of our own. What then? Does God give us any consolation when others have caused our trouble?

Asaph meditated in his heart and made a diligent search. It sounds as though he was content to search within himself. I don't know about you, but for me, this would be scary. To search my own heart for relief is about as frightening as . . . well, as searching my own heart for the words to songs while performing in front of thousands of people. The true ending to my Milwaukee story is that I bombed that night. I was completely out of sync with the band. We made it through, but in my heart I knew that I had let my band members down. No, when I am troubled, I do not want to rely on my own abilities to remember.

By God's grace, we have two things Asaph didn't have. First, we have Jesus' own words. "Let not your hearts be troubled. Believe in God; believe also in Me" (John 14:1). Asaph had the promise of the Messiah to come. You and I have His actual words and deeds recorded in Scripture. Asaph had the promise that God would send the Redeemer. You and I can open the text and read how Jesus fulfilled all that the Law and the prophets had said, and then offered Himself up on the cross for our sins.

Second, we have one who intercedes for us. Paul says to the Romans, "Likewise the Spirit helps us in our weakness. For we do not know what to pray for as we ought, but the Spirit Himself intercedes for us with groanings too deep for words" (Romans 8:26).

The next time you're faced with a troubled heart, as Asaph was, remember that Christ Jesus offers the sure foundation of forgiveness through His death and resurrection. Though there are going to be battles in life that are sure to bring trouble, He has already won the war through His work on the cross. May the Spirit use this knowledge to bring you comfort and peace in troubled times. Amen.

You and I have [Jesus'] actual words and deeds recorded in Scripture. [We] can open the text and read how Jesus fulfilled all that the Law and the prophets had said, and then offered Himself up on the cross for our sins.

Prayer: Lord God, when I am troubled, help me to remember and meditate on the song of Your deliverance through Your Son. By Your Spirit, give me the strength and courage to make it through whatever lies before me. In Jesus' name I pray. Amen.

1. Honestly now; what is the longest time you have spent carefully meditating on God's blessings to you?

2. The psalmist is too disturbed even to speak; in what ways might our busy activity in trying to fix the problems we encounter actually be a poorer response than stunned silence?

3. What value is there in remembering "the days of old"? What are some old memories that can help you as you endure difficult trials?

4. What might Asaph mean by his "song"? If the story of your life's relationship with God was written as a song, what would it sound like?

5. Take five minutes right now and see how many good gifts from God you can remember as part of the story or song that make up your relationship with God.

Psalm 77:7–9

> "Will the Lord spurn forever, and never again be favorable? Has His steadfast love forever ceased? Are His promises at an end for all time? Has God forgotten to be gracious? Has He in anger shut up His compassion?" *Selah*

God Has Not Forgotten

The X-ray images were unmistakable; there was something inside that was not supposed to be there. It was a six-and-a-half-inch surgical clamp, forgotten by a team of surgeons who had performed successful surgery on the patient just two weeks earlier. Well . . . er . . . um . . . somewhat successful surgery. There's no way of knowing exactly how something like this happened. The doctors blamed the nurses, the nurses blamed the doctors; in the end, no one remembered to get that last clamp. How does one miss a six-and-a-half-inch shiny-steel clamp? I probably shouldn't be so accusatory here. My wife is bound to read this and point out that I once looked in the refrigerator and missed a six-inch-wide, ten-inch-tall gallon of milk. But I am not a surgeon.

If you are reading this and you happen to be a surgeon, forgive me for bringing this up. But, the truth is, the rest of us get a great deal of satisfaction out of seeing that even the most educated and gifted individuals on the planet forget things now and then. I realize that this knowledge is only satisfying to those of us who have never had a surgeon leave an implement inside of us. If you have been the unfortunate recipient of a forgotten surgical clamp, I am sorry the rest of us are being satisfied at your expense. By the way, the patient in this story was fine; and the surgeons did agree to go back in and get that last clamp at no charge. Wow, buy-one-get-one-free surgeries!

Forgetfulness is one of those characteristics that can sneak up on you. What I mean is, you can be having a great day and then, in a flash of forgetfulness, you lock your keys in the car or leave your headlights on. Nothing spoils a nice evening out on the town with your wife like returning to a car that either won't start or won't let you in. Forgetfulness is one of my weaknesses. I can prove it by telling you I cannot remember how many times I have locked my keys in the car or left my headlights on.

The question the psalmist asks in these verses is likely a rhetorical one, but it does point out that in our weakness we sometimes project our own failings on God. Because I am forgetful, and God made me, then He must also be forgetful, right? That's not exactly right, though I'll step out on a limb here and say God doesn't remember everything. Perhaps you know that Jeremiah prophesied that God would establish a new covenant with the house of Israel and with the house of Judah. He brings us God's Word, saying, "I will forgive their iniquity, and I will remember their sin no more" (Jeremiah 31:34). Isaiah prophesied similar words in Isaiah 43:25. However, though God does promise to not remember the sins of His people, it would be incorrect to say that He forgets to be gracious. Anyway, not remembering our sin sounds like it goes hand in hand with God's graciousness.

I think the psalmist's words actually reflect feelings that we have all experienced, the feelings of being lost and being alone. Last winter, an ice storm hit northern Indiana, and our power was out for five days. The temperatures plunged, and I worried that our pipes would freeze. Every night, I burned lanterns to keep the house warm.

During the first night, I had a wonderfully peaceful time in the dark, waking up every now and then to check the temperature. No problems, none of the rooms got below 45 degrees. The second night, it was 10 degrees outside. Inside, I burned lanterns and kept it above 40 degrees. The third night is when the real cold hit. It was -12 degrees outside. I fought the cold all night, sleeping only 30 minutes at a time. I found comfort in prayer, knowing that God was hearing my pleas for strength through this difficult time. The temperature in the house was down to 35 degrees in the morning.

During the next day, the temperature outside stayed below zero. I knew it would once again be a long night if the power didn't come on, and I prayed God would give us some relief. The novelty had worn off for my wife and kids, so they packed up and headed to Grandma's house. As the sun went down, I realized relief was not in God's plan just yet.

The temperature outside fell to -23 degrees. I stayed up around the clock, moving lanterns from room to room, spending 15 minutes in each room. The night was almost unbearable. At 2 a.m., the temperature in the house was at 33 degrees. Around 2:30 a.m., I ran out of fuel for the lanterns. I was tired, cold, lonely, and to be honest with you, I was losing touch with what was happening. I had been up for nearly four days straight. I prayed that God would be gracious.

The word "gracious" is such a loaded word, isn't it? Think of the many ways we could question God's graciousness. Has He forgotten that I'm one of His children? Has He forgotten that He loves me? Has he forgotten that He sent His own Son for me? Has He forgotten that I even exist? If all of this is true, then I am lost and alone. Have you ever felt this way? This is how the psalmist was feeling. Where do we go when God seems to have forgotten to be gracious?

The night that I sat in a near-freezing house, I was tired, cold, and lonely because I am human; we tend to get tired, cold, and lonely in these circumstances. Clearly, another human characteristic is forgetfulness. I am forgetful not only with car keys and headlights but also with God's graciousness. But the cross reminds us that God will never forget to be gracious. We have a gracious God who loves us, cares for us, and remembers us.

Men, I want to challenge you today to do something specific. If you find yourself wondering if God has forgotten to be gracious, perhaps you are as forgetful as me. When you find yourself in that situation, meet at the cross and be reminded again about the grace of God. And oh, since you asked, I survived!

....

The cross reminds us that God will never forget to be gracious. We have a gracious God who loves us, cares for us, and remembers us.

Prayer: Blessed Holy Spirit, I confess my forgetfulness in showing love and service to my wife, my kids, my friends, and my employer. Help me to be mindful of their needs, as You are mindful of mine through Your Word. I ask this in Jesus' name. Amen.

....

Wednesday

1. What's the most costly mistake you have made that was the result of nothing more than forgetting something?

2. This short section of the psalm is rhetorically quite powerful as Asaph fires off his salvo of hard questions. What kind of internal tension does this line of interrogation create in you, the twenty-first-century reader?

3. Considering what we know of God's faithfulness, why is it that the questions of these verses can be so troubling, even to a believer?

4. How do you "turn off" the questions about God and His faithfulness that arise when you are slogging through a hard trial?

5. When you look objectively at your life situation, what are the questions that legitimately rise up and demand your attention? How do you answer them?

Psalm 77:10–15

> Then I said, "I will appeal to this, to the years of the right hand of the Most High." I will remember the deeds of the LORD; yes, I will remember Your wonders of old. I will ponder all Your work, and meditate on Your mighty deeds. Your way, O God, is holy. What god is great like our God? You are the God who works wonders; You have made known Your might among the peoples. You with Your arm redeemed Your people, the children of Jacob and Joseph. *Selah*

In the Lord's Might

I don't fancy myself to be a connoisseur of fine art, so you should read this with the understanding that I have had to do my research to write this devotion. I was recently captivated by a painting that was pictured on the cover of a book in the library. It was a depiction of Christ on the cross. His outstretched arms show the details of His tendons and muscles. His head hangs limp, and his gaunt, twisted figure is riddled with thorns and cuts from the scourging He endured at the hands of soldiers. The striking part for me is the Savior's arms. They are stretched up and out at a 45-degree angle as far as they can go, and then curled over the top of the cross and nailed. His upper arms and forearms are punctured with thorns and shards of rock. His lifeless fingers are curled away from the cross and the blood has drained out of them so that they are a ghostly pale.

Matthias Grünewald made the painting on wood panels for the hospital chapel at St. Anthony's Monastery in Isenheim, which was then part of Germany—now in France. The monks at the monastery were known for aiding those who suffered from skin diseases, so Grünewald paid great attention to detail as he painted the stretched and beaten flesh of Christ.

The date was 1515, just two years before Luther nailed the Ninety-five Theses to the Castle Church door in Wittenberg. The painting is commonly referred to as the Isenheim Altarpiece. If you have a computer handy, search for it; I think you will find it worth the effort. If you see it, perhaps you will agree it is an unforgettable painting of Christ on the cross. In the words of our psalm verse for today, this is a painting of the arms of God redeeming His people, the children of Jacob and Joseph.

As men, we tend to equate strength with brute force. But here the psalmist is writing about God redeeming His people simply with His arm. If I were a painter—by the way, this is probably why I'm not a painter—I would paint something like the image on the front of a popular baking soda box, the one with the big, muscular arm holding a huge hammer. Yeah, now that looks powerful. Just imagine that arm winding up and clobbering the sins out of people. However, though that painting could certainly go with this verse, it would not tell the story of God redeeming His people near as well as does Grünewald's painting.

The truth is, the outstretched arm that redeemed God's people was the arm of Christ nailed to the cross. The prophet Isaiah describes that same event in the life of the Savior, "The LORD has bared His holy arm before the eyes of all the nations, and all the ends of the earth shall see the salvation of our God" (Isaiah 52:10). I'm not a fan of everything on the Internet, but if you have already searched and found a picture of the Isenheim Altarpiece, then you have experienced one way that the salvation of our God is literally being seen to the ends of the earth. Images like the Isenheim Altarpiece are wonderful tools of the Gospel because they tell the story. Grünewald's painting has continued to tell the story centuries after his death. I wonder if he could have imagined that five hundred years after he painted it, this altarpiece would still be telling the story of the salvation of our God.

We may not be painters, but there are other ways we can communicate the salvation of our God to the ends of the earth. Believe it or not, the easiest way to proclaim the grace of God to your family is to get them to church. That seems like a simple thing, but as a dad with three kids of my own, I know what a challenge it can be to get everybody up and moving off to worship on a Sunday morning. But it is worth it. When we come to worship and receive God's gifts, we are actually proclaiming the Gospel to the world. The apostle Paul writes, "As often as you eat this bread and drink the cup, you proclaim the Lord's death until He comes" (1 Corinthians 11:26). Taking Communion proclaims the Gospel to your children, not to mention distributing God's forgiveness to you.

Another way to proclaim the Gospel is to lead your family in devotions. I would love to say that this is where I shine at home. Unfortunately, that would not be the whole truth, or even a sliver of the truth. I have tried and failed at family devotions for fifteen years. Lately, though, I've been trying a new approach. Because you are reading this out of a book of devotions, this suggestion is going to sound strange. Rather than reading a prepared devotion, try just reading a Bible story and saying the

Lord's Prayer. I'm convinced that, at my house, starting family devotions is difficult because we are not in the habit of doing it. I can think of no better habit to teach my kids than reading the Bible. Perhaps when we are in the habit of studying God's Word for a few minutes each night, it will be easier to transition to a Bible reading and a prepared devotion. For now, we are focusing on just reading God's Word and praying.

Our devotion time has led to some wonderfully rewarding discussions. I think the best part about being a dad and husband is this kind of dialogue with my wife and kids. I can't trace it back five hundred years, but I can say that for many generations, fathers in my family have enjoyed talking like this with their families. There are no great preachers in my family, just men who lived under God's grace and delighted in sharing that grace with their family.

We have a treasure to share with the world, beginning at home. God has redeemed His people with His arm, His outstretched arm. A painting of Jesus hanging on the cross communicates the Good News that God has redeemed His people. Let's ask God to strengthen us to share the Good News at home.

As men, we tend to equate strength with brute force. But here the psalmist is writing about God redeeming His people simply with His arm.

Prayer: Dear Lord, I confess my weakness and failure to You. Strengthen me so that I might be the man—the husband, father, son, brother, friend—You want me to be. Help me to lead my family, whether large or small, in the righteousness of Your Word. In Jesus' name I pray. Amen.

1. What images or symbols best convey to you the ideas of strength and power?

2. What is the point when the Scriptures speak about God's right hand or His arm?

3. Asaph is taking a stroll down memory lane, with special attention being paid to the times when God worked with His right hand of strength and power for the sake of His people. What would have been some of the highlights in his careful contemplation of this history?

4. How does the right hand of Christ nailed to the cross fit in with the previous images of God's right hand working to save His people?

5. How will remembering God's powerful saving actions make a difference in how you live in the days ahead?

Psalm 77:16–20

> When the waters saw You, O God, when the waters saw You, they were afraid; indeed, the deep trembled. The clouds poured out water; the skies gave forth thunder; Your arrows flashed on every side. The crash of Your thunder was in the whirlwind; Your lightnings lighted up the world; the earth trembled and shook. Your way was through the sea, Your path through the great waters; yet Your footprints were unseen. You led Your people like a flock by the hand of Moses and Aaron.

God's Footprints

As my children sat blindfolded in the back seat, I negotiated the drop-off with the driver and wondered how my wife and I were going to pull off the escape. It was foggy at 5:00 a.m. as we exited the vehicle and entered the airport terminal. Would anyone see us or recognize us? Did the kids have any idea what was going on? I hoped not. Our mission had its origins years earlier. But today, as our blindfolded children were being led through the gate and toward the waiting plane, I wondered, how could it have come to this?

Okay, so that was a suspenseful paragraph, was it not? Becky and I often blindfold our own children and surprise them with fun stuff. The above scenario played out as we were surprising them with a trip to Philadelphia. This family fun began one Valentine's Day, when we blindfolded them and took them out for ice cream. One of the things they like to do afterward is to guess the route we took and then tell us the clues they remember, such as sounds and smells that gave away our position. I'll never forget the morning we surprised them with a ride on the Music City Star, Nashville's commuter train. The sound of that big diesel engine blew the surprise as soon as we pulled into the parking lot.

In our psalm verses for today, we are reminded that God's footprints are often hidden to our eyes, as if we are wearing a blindfold. Sometimes we get a glimpse, after the fact, of God's divine intervention, but He often hides His footprints from us on the shoreline of the sea of life.

When God put the desire to do youth ministry in my heart, I was a fifth- and sixth-grade teacher in Hialeah, Florida. Becky and I decided that I would resign my teaching position at the end of the school year and, in the meantime, look for a position as a youth minister. We hoped to stay in the South, close to those sunny beaches and warm gulf-stream waters. At the end of the school year, having received not even a phone call from any church in Florida, we broke down and interviewed with a congregation in Sheboygan Falls, Wisconsin, not far from the sunny beaches of Lake Michigan. I know, the irony is thick here, isn't it? We laughed at the thought of moving to Wisconsin from South Florida. While we were laughing, God was making invisible footprints in our lives.

Our lease was almost up, so we began packing, though we were unsure as to where we would end up. We already felt God's tug toward the church in Sheboygan Falls, but because we hadn't heard from them, we were quietly hoping a warmer option would come along. Just one week before the move, a church in St. Louis called and expressed an interest in meeting with us. Great! We made plans to go there for an interview on our way to . . . wherever we were moving . . . maybe there.

When moving day arrived, I went to pick up the rental truck, and the nice lady behind the counter asked a simple question, "Where will you be dropping this truck off next week?" "Ummm," I replied; "do you need to know that today?" She was not impressed with my leap of faith. "Well, that would be nice!" she said rather sarcastically. I agreed it would, in fact, be real nice to know where I was going, but that was a footprint God was keeping hidden. She forced my hand when she said, "Sir, the computer won't let me check the truck out to you unless you tell me where you are going to return it." Think fast, Steve, where are you going? Since we were planning to interview with the church in St. Louis, I made a quick decision. "St. Louis," I said, "we're going to St. Louis." I didn't really want to end up in cold and snowy Wisconsin anyway. Besides, Becky and I were both born in St. Louis, so this would be a fitting place to settle down and raise kids. She finished the paperwork for one 14-foot truck to be dropped off in St. Louis in seven days. After a few minutes, a worker entered and told her the bad news, there were no 14-foot trucks on the lot. "Sir," she said, "if you're willing, I can rent you a 17-foot truck for the price of a 14-footer." "Great! By the way," I said, "on the off chance that we return the truck in . . . say . . . Milwaukee, what would be the extra charge?" After a brief but entertaining discussion, she added Milwaukee as a potential drop-off site and some extra mileage. I headed home with a 17-foot truck. Here's the part of the story where God finally reveals a footprint. We packed that 17-foot truck so tightly that one of us had to push things in while the other rolled down the door. Even the front seat was full. There is no way we could have packed everything in a 14-foot truck. Thank You, Lord.

We drove to St. Louis for my interview, hoping we could put an end to this craziness. The church in St. Louis was very nice, but God had already been laying footprints for us somewhere else. We realized that Sheboygan Falls was exactly what we were hoping for, of course minus the warm and sunny beaches. The next day, I received a call to be youth minister at St. Paul Lutheran Church in Sheboygan Falls.

Though in the midst of life it can be hard to distinguish God's footprints from others, when we look back we can see that He has indeed led us through the sea. I have been a Christian recording artist for fifteen years. It was the members of St. Paul Lutheran who encouraged me to record some of my own songs, and it was in Wisconsin that people first bought my music and paid me to sing at special events. We spent eight wonderful years in Sheboygan Falls, and when we announced that we would be moving to Nashville and starting a full-time music ministry, the members of St. Paul insisted that we were not leaving, but we were being sent as music missionaries. Do you see the impressions of God's footprints in my life?

Look back on your own life. Do you see how God's footprints have led you through the sea? Hey, why not blindfold your family and take them out for ice cream this week? While you're eating, tell them about God's footprints. They may need you to show them where He has been walking so that their faith might be strengthened. I pray that in the midst of life's challenges you will lead your family to the cross of Jesus, from where your salvation comes, and there you will see how God's footprints, though sometimes unseen, have provided safe passage for you and your family.

Though, in the midst of life it can be hard to distinguish God's footprints from others, when we look back we can see that He has indeed led us through the sea.

Prayer: Dear Lord, through Your Word and Spirit, help me to trust You even when I cannot see with my eyes what You are doing in and through my life. Lead me and be with me as You were with the saints of old. I ask this in Jesus' name. Amen.

1. What, exactly, is Asaph so dramatically and vividly describing in these verses?

2. How might one understand the assertion of verse 19, that God's "way was through the sea"?

3. Why is the recognition that God's ways (His footprints!) are, from a human perspective, often quite unknowable both confounding and consoling?

4. In what sense is it still true to say that God's way of saving His people is "through the sea"?

5. How will you follow God's way today, when His footprints remain hidden?

Week Three

....

Psalm 77

The 77th psalm is a psalm of instruction. The
psalmist uses himself as an example of how
to find comfort when affliction comes and
the conscience is troubled, as if God is angry
with it. He says that he was so troubled that
he could not have any sleep or even speak. But
this comfort follows: The psalmist can fight off
the thoughts with which he futilely suffered,
and he can grasp instead the thought of the
mighty works of God in the histories of old.
Here we find that God's work was to help the
miserable, the troubled, and the abandoned,
and to throw down the self-secure, proud
scoffer, for example, when He delivered the
children of Israel from Egypt.
For this reason His paths are called "hidden."
He is there to help when we think that we are
totally abandoned. We should learn this well.
God intends by this psalm to show us and teach
us His manner of helping, namely that He never
abandons us when things go ill. Instead, we
should wait upon His help at that time with
the greatest confidence and not believe our
thoughts.

-Martin Luther

Week Three, Psalm 77
GROUP BIBLE STUDY
(Questions and answers are on pp. 195–97.)

1. Was the past week one marked with a "day of trouble"? Tell the group about the greatest difficulty you faced this week.

2. The psalmist says an odd thing in verse 3: that when he remembers God, he is disturbed. How can this be? Shouldn't remembering God bring joy and hope?

3. An inability to sleep is a typical corollary of trying times. The psalmist blames his insomnia on God (v. 4). Is this evidence of great faith or proof of little faith?

4. The psalmist seems to engage in a healthy amount of reflection and meditation. What things get in the way of Christians emulating this practice of careful reflection and meditation?

5. What sort of things should a person think about when he is meditating? What's the difference between meditating and "thinking hard"? Are there any dangers in devoting significant time to meditation?

6. Asaph fires off some rather pointed and perhaps even irreverent questions. What's the difference between these questions and the sort of questions asked by antagonistic unbelievers? Are there any questions that a believer should not ask God, even rhetorically?

7. In verse 13, Asaph reminds us that God's way is holy. What does an emphasis on God's holy ways help us understand about God's way of doing things?

8. Why is a historical review of God's saving work (vv. 10–20) of such value to the psalmist in dealing with his difficult situation? What can the Church do to help its people to be better equipped to do the kind of remembering that Asaph finds so helpful?

9. The struggle of Asaph seems to be quite personal, yet he finds hope and comfort by recalling God's actions for the whole people of Israel. What role does the Church (God's flock) play in an individual Christian's wrestling with life?

10. The psalm provides a great defense and example of the value that remembering has in the life of a believer. What are some of the significant memories that your group would include in a compilation of "holy events" that demonstrate God's faithfulness to His people as He fulfills His promise to save?

Week Four

Psalm 80

[1] Give ear, O Shepherd of Israel, You who lead Joseph like a flock! You who are enthroned upon the cherubim, shine forth.

[2] Before Ephraim and Benjamin and Manasseh, stir up Your might and come to save us!

[3] Restore us, O God; let Your face shine, that we may be saved!

[4] O Lord God of hosts, how long will You be angry with Your people's prayers?

[5] You have fed them with the bread of tears and given them tears to drink in full measure.

[6] You make us an object of contention for our neighbors, and our enemies laugh among themselves.

[7] Restore us, O God of hosts; let Your face shine, that we may be saved!

[8] You brought a vine out of Egypt; you drove out the nations and planted it.

[9] You cleared the ground for it; it took deep root and filled the land.

[10] The mountains were covered with its shade, the mighty cedars with its branches.

¹¹ It sent out its branches to the sea
and its shoots to the River.

¹² Why then have you broken down its walls, so that
all who pass along the way pluck its fruit?

¹³ The boar from the forest ravages it,
and all that move in the field feed on it.

¹⁴ Turn again, O God of hosts! Look down from
heaven, and see; have regard for this vine,

¹⁵ the stock that Your right hand planted, and for
the son whom You made strong for yourself.

¹⁶ They have burned it with fire; they have cut it
down; may they perish at the rebuke of Your face!

¹⁷ But let Your hand be on the man of Your right hand,
the son of man whom You have made strong for Yourself!

¹⁸ Then we shall not turn back from You;
give us life, and we will call upon Your name!

¹⁹ Restore us, O Lord God of hosts!
Let Your face shine, that we may be saved!

Gary Dunker

Psalm 80:1–3

> Give ear, O Shepherd of Israel, You who lead Joseph like a flock! You who are enthroned upon the cherubim, shine forth. Before Ephraim and Benjamin and Manasseh, stir up Your might and come to save us! Restore us, O God; let Your face shine, that we may be saved!

Sheep Stink; God Saves

Everything I know about sheep I've learned on two occasions: once when I was five, and a second time only a few weeks ago. Years ago, my kindergarten class took a field trip to a farm owned by our teacher. There I learned at a very early age that sheep stink. A few weeks ago, I learned that sheep actually respond to the voice of their shepherd. I learned this lesson while listening to a Christian writer describe his trip to Israel. What he said surprised me. He told the story of how he watched two Bedouin shepherds stopping in a field to talk. As they conversed, their sheep intermingled. When the shepherds were finished, one let out a command and began walking away. Instantly, his sheep separated themselves from the other flock and followed after their shepherd. With those two events in mind, let's spend some time in Asaph's psalm.

Frankly, you and I stink. Nothing personal—it's just that our rebellion against God causes a bad odor. If the wages of sin is death, as Paul tells us in Romans 6:23a, then sin causes us to smell rotten. So are we really sheep? Isaiah, one of Israel's greatest prophets, used the word *sheep* to describe human beings. See if this fits you and me: "All we like sheep have gone astray; we have turned—every one—to his own way" (Isaiah 53:6). As smelly sheep, guys, we tend to intermingle with other smelly sheep. Don't we gravitate around the water coolers of our lives—the golf courses, the board rooms, the coffee shops—and talk about the cute secretary in the cubicle next to ours, brag about the big raise we just got, or boast in how much alcohol we can handle? Face it; we're smelly sheep in need of a shepherd to bathe us and lead us down another path.

Throughout history, God has called His people to follow Him. Maybe you remember the story of the exodus from Egypt. At that time, God's people responded to their Shepherd's call through Moses. Under Joshua, God called His sheep to follow Him through the Jordan River and into the Promised Land. They did, and the fortified city of Jericho fell before them and they conquered the land. Once a little boy named Samuel heard God's voice in the night and responded, "Speak, LORD, for Your servant hears" (1 Samuel 3:10). Samuel followed God and grew to crown both Saul and David as kings of Israel.

What do you think: Does God still call stinky sheep today or has Asaph taken us down a dead-end road with this psalm? Listen to the words of Jesus in John's Gospel:

> "My sheep hear My voice, and I know them, and they follow Me. I give them eternal life, and they will never perish, and no one will snatch them out of My hand. My Father, who has given them to Me, is greater than all, and no one is able to snatch them out of the Father's hand. I and the Father are one." (John 10:27-30)

The event that Asaph points us to in Psalm 80 is likely the destruction of the Northern Kingdom by the Assyrians. The future looked bleak, but the Shepherd of Israel, He who was enthroned above the cherubim and who distributed mercy from the blood-sprinkled mercy seat, the golden lid of the ark of the covenant, could be trusted.

Do you hear the voice of Jesus calling you out from among the other smelly sheep? He has, and He does through His Word! He has already bathed you in the water of your Baptism (Romans 6:1-4). At that time, God set His Spirit within you. It's the Spirit who causes your ears to perk up whenever you hear God calling your name through the Word. Through His precious Word, He calls you to follow Him, just like Jesus said to His disciples, "Come, follow Me!" While we follow Him, He sustains us along the way. He feeds us with His body and blood in Holy Communion. Real food, "given and shed *for you* for the forgiveness of your sins."

God leads us by His Son in human flesh. This is Jesus, who proclaimed, "I am the good shepherd. I know My own and My own know me, just as the Father knows Me and I know the Father; and I lay down My life for the sheep" (John 10:14). Jesus calls you and me to lead our families in faith. We're not called to sit passively in our pews; rather, God enables us to bless and influence the lives of others. What a glorious story we have to tell of the Shepherd who leads stinky sheep to eternal life! Asaph knew Him, God's Old Testament people knew Him, and we know Him too. This Shepherd alone has the power to save us, and He has, through His cross. He Himself is our eternal mercy seat (ESV: "propitiation"; Romans 3:25).

By His mighty hand, God led His covenant people out of Egypt and into the Promised Land. God will lead us, His new covenant people, into eternal life. God's only Son, the Good Shepherd, has called us to follow Him. Through the power of His Holy Spirit, God speaks to each of us that He has come to save us in Jesus Christ and that He has restored us to Himself and shines His face upon us—His everlasting love and grace.

By His mighty hand, God led His covenant people out of Egypt and into the Promised Land. God will lead us, His new covenant people, into eternal life.

Prayer: Faithful Shepherd, enable me to lead my family both physically and spiritually according to Your will. Help me to speak Your Word to those in my life, so that more sheep might be brought into Your fold. I ask this in Your name. Amen.

Monday

1. Do you take exception to being likened to a sheep, or does the image encourage you?

2. What does the phrase "enthroned upon the cherubim" actually mean?

3. God as leader (shepherd) and God as Lord (enthroned) are two distinct images used to invoke God's intervention for His people. Which one most resonates with you? Why?

4. How much difference does a "shining" face or countenance make?

5. Are you experiencing God more as Lord or as shepherd? Do you see His face shining, or is there darkness in the glance of God today?

Psalm 80:4-7

> O LORD God of hosts, how long will You be angry with Your people's prayers? You have fed them with the bread of tears and given them tears to drink in full measure. You make us an object of contention for our neighbors, and our enemies laugh among themselves. Restore us, O God of hosts; let Your face shine, that we may be saved!

Let Your Face Shine

Boy, does this psalm fit me. How about you? Ever had a time in your life when you've prayed and come up empty? By that I mean, have you prayed and then thought your prayer was unanswered? God's people did. In fact, according to Asaph, after the Assyrians overran the Northern Kingdom, the Israelites prayed and prayed and prayed. Tears streamed down their faces in anguish. They cried not once or twice, but over and over again. Their entire diet consisted of tears for bread and for drink (quite the high-salt, low-calorie diet). Time after time, these refugees from the North humbled themselves before God: "Restore us, O God of hosts!" Yet it seemed to them that their words fell on deaf ears, although those ears belonged to God. Have you ever felt that hopeless? I know I have.

I've told this to several of my friends, and those who know me chuckle, but it's true—I have no patience. If asked to name one thing I have repeatedly prayed for over the past ten years, I'd have to say that it is patience: patience in raising my children, patience while waiting for God to open new career paths, patience for just about everything. Patience. Patience. Patience. The best analogy for my impatience comes in the form of a cartoon I saw a few years ago. In this cartoon, the artist has placed two vultures in a tree that stands in the middle of a desert. The caption is simple, yet poignant: "Patience??? No, I'm going to kill something." Does that fit you? It certainly fits me. My wife likes to say that my favorite prayer is, "Lord, give me patience. NOW!!"

Not only does this sound like me but you might think it also sounds a bit like Asaph and God's people in this psalm. Sure, it evens sounds a bit like David. Although David was an extraordinary man, he was also human. David struggled. He had problems in his life. He had enemies. He suffered defeats. He knew worry. He had problems with his kids. He even had an extramarital affair that cost him an infant son. But in spite of it all, Scripture never indicates that he ever stopped loving God and believing that God would hear and answer his prayers in God's own time and way, at least not for any extended length of time.

Everyone, including God's Old Testament people, struggle with impatience. But there's a difference between struggling with something and allowing Satan tempt you into rank disbelief: believing that God doesn't hear your prayers and won't ever respond. We shouldn't read this psalm and think that God's people lacked faith. No; even when their world had collapsed around them, even though God seemed "angry" with their prayers, they still came to Him. That's what makes the psalms in this book so special. These are "lament" psalms, psalms of God's people crying out to Him in distress. It was so bad for God's people that even the unbelieving nations bordering Israel mocked their faith in God (v. 6). It may be that unbelievers mock you because they know what's going on in your life and choose to taunt you. Certainly, unbelievers have mocked me. When I've mentioned that I continually pray for patience, they fire back, "Like that's ever going to happen!"

Want a good antidote to impatience? Look to Jesus' instruction on prayer. Jesus gave us a model prayer in the Lord's Prayer, which He lived out in His own life. Jesus taught us to pray, "Our Father in heaven, hallowed be Your name. Your kingdom come, *Your will be done*, on earth as it is in heaven. Give us this day our daily bread, and forgive us our debts, as we also have forgiven our debtors. And lead us not into temptation, but deliver us from evil" (Matthew 6:9–13). Note the italicized words. For us, these four words are an outward response to the inward faith worked by the Holy Spirit, working through the Gospel, in our lives. In them, we are saying to God, "Lord, I trust You. I concede my will to Your will. Look at what's happening to me, help me, and hear my prayer for Your sake." Sounds a lot like Asaph's prayer in today's psalm, doesn't it?

Let's travel with Jesus to the Garden of Gethsemane for a moment. *Gethsemane* means "oil press," and in Jesus' prayer on the Mount of Olives we can see how Jesus felt pressed in on all sides. Matthew's Gospel records that Jesus prayed these words twice as He looked His own death and the hell He would face on the cross: "My Father, if it be possible, let this cup pass from Me" (Matthew 26:39, 42). Doesn't this remind you of the tortured anguish that Asaph expresses in Psalm 80 and the same anguish we sometimes feel too? Jesus turned His life over to God, trusting Him for deliverance, "Not as I will, but as You will" (Matthew 26:39, 42).

Your will be done.

The cup of redemption that Jesus offers us through His Gospel cost Him the cup of suffering that He drank in full on the cross: God's full wrath, wrath that we deserve. Leaving Gethsemane, Jesus would face the mockery, the beatings, the false testimonies, and the agony of the cross; but beyond that, His resurrection and His ascension into heaven. Because of Jesus, we can pray with Asaph, "Restore us, O God of hosts; let Your face shine, that we may be saved!" (v. 7). The Gospel of God's forgiveness in Christ renews our faith so that, even in the midst of our tears, we can be confident in God's love and mercy.

There's a lesson for you and me in Asaph's psalm. Others have felt what we feel. Although they stumbled and fell in their walk with the Lord, some of Israel never lost hope. They looked to the salvation that only God can bring. Jesus accomplished that for us. Paul wrote, "For while we were still weak, at the right time Christ died for the ungodly" (Romans 5:6). At the right time. The Lord will restore us, His face will shine on us, and He will save us, all at the right time.

Lord, we pray, Thy will be done.

Although they stumbled and fell in their walk with the Lord, some of Israel never lost hope. They looked to the salvation that only God can bring. Jesus accomplished that for us.

Prayer: Dear God, when I am down, comfort me with the sure knowledge that You have forgiven my sins for Jesus' sake. Help me to trust in the promises You make to me in Your Word. And in all things, O Lord, Your will be done. In Jesus' name. Amen.

Daily Study Questions
Psalm 80:4-7

1. How does Asaph know that God is angry with the prayers of His people?

2. Have you ever been so distressed by a situation that it moved you to tears and made it impossible to eat?

3. Where does Asaph place the blame for the sorrow and agony of the people for whom he cares?

4. Who are your enemies, and what would move them to laughter at your expense?

5. What does it mean to call the Lord the "God of hosts." Why is it fitting in this psalm?

Psalm 80:8–13

> You brought a vine out of Egypt; You drove out the nations and planted it. You cleared the ground for it; it took deep root and filled the land. The mountains were covered with its shade, the mighty cedars with its branches. It sent out its branches to the sea and its shoots to the River. Why then have You broken down its walls, so that all who pass along the way pluck its fruit? The boar from the forest ravages it, and all that move in the field feed on it.

Our True Vine

My wife has the most wonderful recipe for rhubarb bread pudding. It's a recipe handed down from her mother, and one my wife has prepared faithfully for years. My mother-in-law used lots of rhubarb when it was in season. Although she made rhubarb syrup, rhubarb/strawberry jam, and rhubarb pie, she always made rhubarb bread pudding first. My father-in-law called it a "spring tonic." Start with two cups of rhubarb in a greased baking dish. Add several slices of bread and sugar. Over this, pour a mixture of eggs, sugar, and milk. Top with marshmallows and butter. Bake for 45 minutes, and what's not to love? If you're wondering what this has to do with Psalm 80, I beg your indulgence. I want to share with you a bit about rhubarb so that I can share something with you about God's vine.

When my wife and I moved back to Nebraska a few years ago, we were pleased to see that part of our yard, near the southwest corner of our house, supported two rhubarb plants. The plants' location allowed for ample sunlight and nutrition. Over the next few years, we began our own springtime ritual. As soon as a few stalks grew to the correct size, we pulled them and made rhubarb bread pudding. Even my father-in-law commented on how delicious our rhubarb tasted. Yet, danger—an oak tree—lurked nearby and we didn't even know it. Over time, the oak tree grew, sending its roots to roam near the surface of the ground and gathering nutrients from the soil to feed itself. The oak's leafy branches soon blocked the sun that once shone on our precious rhubarb plants. One summer, our rhubarb came through the ground as usual, but instead of maturing into red stalks of succulent delight, it became spindly and inedible.

Let's look at Psalm 80. A vine that had once flourished had now lost its defenses and been destroyed, seemingly eaten alive by a wild animal. Here, Asaph is talking about how God had carefully transplanted His people ("a vine"; v. 8) out of Egypt and had given them the Promised Land. God had cared for them there. Because of His continual blessing, even foreign nations ("the mountains"; v. 10) were influenced by Israel. Israel had spread out from the Mediterranean Sea to the Jordan River (v. 11). But now, with its defenses shattered ("broken down its walls"; v. 12), the land was being ravaged ("pluck its fruit"; v. 12), most notably by the Assyrians ("the boar from the forest"; v. 13).

We should note that God caused Assyria to invade the Northern Kingdom because of His people's sin. God is not capricious; He doesn't punish for pleasure. Rather, He disciplines His children so that they will repent of their sin and turn to Him in faith. Like the oak tree in my rhubarb story, sin takes root a little at a time until it crowds out the spiritual nutrients God desires for our maturity. Sin causes us to become "spindly" Christians. In fact, sin produces more sin and just makes the situation all the worse. Just as the roots of that oak tree stole vital nutrients from my rhubarb plants and the oak tree's leafy canopy robbed my rhubarb of life-giving sunshine, sin steals vital spiritual nutrients—God's grace and mercy—and life-giving Sonshine.

My wife and I made a critical diagnosis: a transplant was needed for our rhubarb to survive. Our search for better soil and less shade led us to a plot of ground in the southeast corner of our yard. After removing a few shovelfuls of dirt, we planned a fall transplant. Then we carefully dug around our dormant rhubarb and placed it in its new location—fertilizing and watering it so that it might take root in the spring. Under the advice of my father (another rhubarb fan), we planned not to pull any rhubarb for an entire growing season, allowing the plant to adjust to its new environment. The following spring, we watched as the transplanted stalks burst forth. Through the spring, it continued growing. One spring Sunday, my father and I walked around the south side of the house. He looked at the rhubarb and asked, "Is this rhubarb the one you transplanted last fall?" I told him that it was. He replied, "Normally, I'd tell you to leave the plant alone for an entire growing season, but in this case, help yourself. The stalks look healthy enough to harvest; you don't need to wait any longer."

Recall again what God did in the life of His Old Testament people, which Asaph recalls in this psalm. God transplanted His people from Egypt to the Promised Land, where she flourished. Then their faith flagged and they turned to worshiping other gods. God allowed Israel and Judah to be invaded. Yet God did not abandon His people in their sin; rather, He transplanted them into Assyria and Babylon. Those who remained strong in faith, He brought back to Israel. Through this faithful remnant, God brought forth His promised Messiah, His own Son, Jesus Christ. (Asaph even hints at Jesus with the phrase "son of man" in v. 17.) Jesus was born to the Virgin Mary, lived a life of perfect obedience to God for us, died the death we deserved, and rose to grant eternal life to all those who repent and believe in Him.

This is the same Jesus Christ, the Son of Man, who proclaimed, "I am the vine; you are the branches. Whoever abides in Me and I in him, he it is that bears much fruit, for apart from Me you can do nothing" (John 15:5). Asaph's psalm, while speaking to the history of God's Old Testament people following the Assyrian invasion, also points us to Jesus Christ, the true Vine. Through the Gospel, God both gives and nourishes our faith. Faith, according to the author of Hebrews, "is the assurance of things hoped for, the conviction of things not seen" (11:1). Even when the situation is lamentable (withering rhubarb plants certainly don't compare to being invaded, but you see my point), we are never without hope. Connected to the true Vine through faith, God will see us through.

Asaph's psalm, while speaking to the history of God's Old Testament people following the Assyrian invasion, also points us to Jesus Christ, the true Vine.

Prayer: Lord Jesus Christ, thank You for connecting me to You through faith, and for joining me to Your death and resurrection in Baptism. When God disciplines me, never let me lose hope, for I know that You give me eternal life. I ask this in Your name. Amen.

1. Why might someone (you or maybe someone you know) find great satisfaction in yard work and gardening?

2. The psalmist moves to his second agrarian image for the Church. What connections can you draw between a grape vine and God's Church?

3. Asaph tells the story of the exodus, using the image of the vine. Keeping that imagery in play, what does he mean in verse 12 with the reference to a broken wall and the vine's fruit being consumed by passersby?

4. How does Asaph demonstrate his unwavering faith in God?

5. The vine, Israel, took deep root in the land. What can you do today to put your own roots a bit deeper into the land God has prepared for you?

Psalm 80:14–18

> Turn again, O God of hosts! Look down from heaven, and see; have regard for this vine, the stock that Your right hand planted, and for the son whom You made strong for Yourself. They have burned it with fire; they have cut it down; may they perish at the rebuke of Your face! But let Your hand be on the man of Your right hand, the son of man whom You have made strong for Yourself! Then we shall not turn back from You; give us life, and we will call upon Your name!

Give Us Life

Tiny scratches on my arms and hands bear witness to my struggle. No matter how careful I am, I always find myself nursing wounds from each encounter. Every spring, pruning rosebushes occupies at least one Saturday morning. As the sun warms the earth, my wife and I watch for signs that our rosebushes have "wintered" successfully. Green growth up the rose branches indicates that our roses have survived and should continue to grow and bloom. We watch as the green growth moves further up. As it does, we begin the process of trimming away the dead branches, leaving only the healthy branches. If the green fades or disappears altogether, we know that we'll need to buy a replacement. In that case, we dig up the dead rosebush and plant its replacement where the dead rose once stood.

In our text from Psalm 80 today, God has given Asaph a glimpse into the future. Asaph foretells a pivotal point in Israel's history. Like a rose, God planted Israel in the Promised Land with His right hand. There she flourished in her season, but she didn't "winter" well. Idolatry and immorality crept in and, like the frigid winds of winter, stole life from the rose God's hand planted. In the spring, God searched His rose for signs of life. Finding little to save, He began trimming away dead branches. But the verses for today offer glimmers of hope. Asaph prays, "Turn again . . . look down . . . see . . . have regard" (v. 14). People who turn to God with their laments and complaints in the midst of calamity are not demonstrating a weak constitution (although this is what the world thinks). Rather, they are demonstrating a strong faith.

Like the dead branches on my rosebushes, sin must be dealt with. God trims away our unfruitful thoughts, words, and deeds in His discipline. Some Christians look at God's discipline as punishment, but that's an inappropriate word; the correct word is *discipline*. Note the words of Hebrews 12:5–6, "My son, do not regard lightly the discipline of the Lord, nor be weary when reproved by Him. For the Lord disciplines the one He loves, and chastises every son whom He receives." God disciplines those He loves but He laid the punishment of sin on His own Son. "But He [Jesus Christ] was wounded for our transgressions; He was crushed for our iniquities; upon Him was the chastisement that brought us peace, and with His stripes we are healed" (Isaiah 53:5).

Although this psalm speaks to the Northern Kingdom following its fall to Assyria, the Southern Kingdom would also fall, but to Babylon. Even while exiled, there was a faithful remnant who continued to worship the God of creation. Members of this faithful remnant returned from captivity to rebuild Jerusalem and the temple that Solomon built. Through this faithful remnant (the seemingly dead root of the rose), God brought Jesus Christ. Even though Judah was reduced to the "stump of Jesse" (Isaiah 11:1, 10), God brought out of that stump a shoot that greened and grew to full maturity. This "stump of Jesse" is Jesus, "the man of Your [God's] right hand, the son of man whom You have made strong for Yourself!" (Psalm 80:17).

How does this relate to you and me? There may be times in our lives when sin reduces us to a near-dead root. Our faith no longer puts forth copious green branches filled with love for God and love for our fellow man. God looks at our lives and, as a skilled gardener does each spring, begins trimming away the dead branches by means of His righteous discipline. Sometimes this may result in our "hitting rock bottom." Isn't it amazing that when you "hit rock bottom," the only place to look is up? By God's righteous pruning, soon only the stump remains. Then, through His Word, spoken by our pastor or a Christian family member or friend, He sends the Holy Spirit deep into our lives and life begins anew, like a wintered rose. God restores us to our Baptism, when our old man drowned and our new man arose to take its place (Romans 6:3–4).

God not only desires but also effects repentance in our lives. God's discipline leads to repentance, just as my wife and I trim away dead branches of our rosebushes each spring to let new growth come forth. Seldom does this trimming come without some pain or discomfort. In the case of David and his extra-marital affair with Bathsheba, God's pruning brought calamity and cost him a son (2 Samuel 12:11, 14). Although God pruned him, through Nathan's ministry God also restored David to His grace, forgiveness, and eternal life. God likewise forgave and ultimately restored His people in the Promised Land, so that they could again worship Him and receive the promised Messiah.

Through the Gospel, God revives our faith, causing it to "green up" and mature. St. Paul puts it this way, "But when the goodness and loving kindness of God our Savior appeared, He saved us, not because of works done by us in righteousness, but according to His own mercy, by the washing of regeneration and renewal of the Holy Spirit, whom He poured out on us richly through Jesus Christ our Savior, so that being justified by His grace we might become heirs according to the hope of eternal life" (Titus 3:4–7). Connected to Jesus, you are "right" with God and have the promise of eternal life.

Pruning affords an effective way of aiding roses to grow; so too, the discipline God brings into our lives aids our faith to grow. But, like Asaph in today's psalm verses, what encourages us and brings us through is trust in God's right-hand man, the Son of Man, whom God made strong for Himself (Psalm 80:15, 17).

....

[God's] discipline leads to repentance, just as my wife and I trim away dead branches of our rosebushes each spring to let new growth come forth.

Prayer: Heavenly Father, it seems as though I stray from You and Your Word each day. Please forgive me, and help me to accept Your loving discipline in my life as You conform me to the image of Your Son. In His name I pray. Amen.

....

1. How might this portion of the psalm be understood in the sense of a child's appeal for parental help?

2. The psalm makes another turn to a still deeper image, identifying the vine with a chosen son. Who is this special, "right hand" Son of God?

3. Earlier, the psalmist had prayed for God's face to shine on the people (v. 3). The alternative is not pleasant. What happens when God's look carries a rebuke?

4. Notice that this chosen son of man is clearly established by God to accomplish God's purpose (v. 17). How does this understanding of God's work bring comfort to a vine (or a nation or a person) who has been cut down to the ground?

5. What do these verses teach you about the things you seek from God and the way that you ask of God?

Psalm 80:19

> Restore us, O LORD God of hosts! Let Your face shine, that we may be saved!

Fixers

God wired men differently than woman; guys, we're fixers. What I mean is that, when a problem arises, we're right in there. Change the tire. Change the oil. Unblock the toilet. Replace the garbage disposal. Replace the light bulb. We're on it in a heartbeat, right? But let's be honest; aren't there times when being a fixer doesn't matter? As much as we want to "fix" certain situations—relationships, kids, the workplace environment, our employment, aging and dependant parents—there are times when we are unable to make any sort of improvement at all. Sure, the old adage is that when you reach the bottom of your rope you tie a knot in it and hang on, but how realistic is that? I don't know about you, but if I hold onto a rope for long enough, knot or no, my palms get sweaty and I lose my grip and fall.

When we read our Bibles, we have a tendency to think of biblical characters as superheroes, and that somehow we'll never measure up to them or how they handled situations. Do you know any men who believe that? Let's review Psalm 80 and see if that holds true. Keep in mind that this is not a boastful puff-piece; it's a psalm of lament. In verse 1, Asaph calls on the Shepherd of Israel to hear him. In verse 3, he asks God to restore him. In verse 4, he appeals to the Lord of hosts to tell him how long He will stay angry and not answer his prayers. In verse 7, Asaph asks for restoration from the God of hosts. He pleads to the Lord God of hosts in verses 14 and 19. That's six appeals (if my math is correct) in nineteen verses, all to God. What that tells us is that Asaph knows that the only reliable source to fix the unfixable is God. Of his own strength, Asaph cannot hold onto the knotted rope anymore than you or I can. I'm going to sneak another question in here: If we *could* "fix" every situation, to whom would the glory belong? To us. The more we believe that we can solve our own problems, the more self-centered and less God- or Christ-centered we become. Clearly, Asaph is neither a fixer nor a superhero.

However, in Psalm 80, Asaph points us heavenward to the true source of our salvation. Let's try our experiment one more time, going further back in time, back to when the young shepherd boy David faced giant Goliath, and we'll see how a real man fixed things.

Standing nine feet nine inches tall, Goliath could just barely fit under a basketball hoop if he were alive today. Each day, Goliath stepped out in front of the Philistine army to curse God. When David came to visit his brothers, he heard Goliath and asked, "Are you going to do something about that cursing?" His brothers told him to go home. King Saul said, "If you think you can shut Goliath up, have at it. Get the job done and I'll let you marry my daughter." Now, there's a payoff Saul never expected to have to make. All eyes were fixed on David as he bent down to gather some stones for his slingshot. Was everyone doubled over in laughter? Probably. Goliath cursed David, so he answered, "You come to me with a sword and with a spear and with a javelin, but I come to you in the name of the LORD of hosts, the God of the armies of Israel, whom you have defied. This day the LORD will deliver you into my hand, and I will strike you down and cut off your head. And I will give the dead bodies of the host of the Philistines this day to the birds of the air and to the wild beasts of the earth, that all the earth may know that there is a God in Israel, and that all this assembly may know that the LORD saves not with sword and spear" (1 Samuel 17:45–47). Did you get that, "that all the earth may know that there is a God in Israel" and that everyone will know that He does not save with sword and spear. God saves! There is no "I'm David; look what I can do" in this text. Look what God can do! Do you lose sight of that when troubles surround you? I know I do. I do, because I'm a fixer!

Yahweh Sabaoth. Translated from the Hebrew, that means "Lord of hosts" in Psalm 80 and elsewhere in the Bible. We might say "Commander of all the armies of heaven." Asaph's plea in verse 19, "Restore us, O LORD God of hosts!" resounds into God's presence. Asaph is using God's personal, covenant name, Yahweh (LORD), and then ascribing to Him ultimate power and authority over all things. Truly, it takes a strong man, a man of faith, to plead to God for salvation. When God turns His face toward us, we are saved!

I have no idea what circumstances you face. But what I do know is that your confidence for eternal salvation rests on the outstretched arms of Jesus Christ. I plan to go back to Psalm 80 every time I think about tying a knot in the end of my rope. Jesus Christ, whom Asaph knew by faith, is our salvation. God's Spirit calls to us to put our trust in Him, the Lord of hosts! He will never leave us or forsake us! For some things, God gives us the grace and abilities to handle. But we don't have to fix everything. We can leave it in His capable hands.

Jesus Christ, whom Asaph knew by faith, is our salvation. God's Spirit calls to us to put our trust in Him, the Lord of hosts! He will never leave us or forsake us.

Prayer: Dear Holy Spirit, free me from the temptation of thinking that I have control over everything in my life. You know I'm no superhero. Through Your Word, strengthen my faith so that I trust God's mercy through His Son, Jesus Christ. I ask this in His name. Amen.

1. When was a time that you tried to "tie a knot" in the end of your rope rather than admit your inability and throw yourself on the mercy of God?

2. Why is it that people (especially men?) would rather tie a knot and keep hanging on than turn to God for everything?

3. How might it be possible to ask for God's help without actually relying on Him completely for the hoped-for deliverance?

4. Notice, again, that Asaph prays in the context of his community. What does your church need that only God can give? When did you last pray for that?

5. What will you do today to cultivate in your life that Christian sense of total reliance on God alone for all that you need?

Week Four

....

Psalm 80

The 80th psalm is a psalm of prayer against the constant enemies, the neighboring people, the Philistines, Syrians, Moabites, and Edomites, who surrounded the people of Israel, pestering and attacking them. So now also we pray against our enemies and neighbors, the rebellious spirits, and the spiritual "fathers" and order, as we have prayed in times past against the heretics of the Church.

-Martin Luther

Week Four, Psalm 80
GROUP BIBLE STUDY
(Questions and answers are on pp. 202–5.)

1. Have you ever heard a prayer that sounded more like a sermon? What's the right balance between keeping a prayer succinct and direct and pouring out a poetic exhortation that recounts most of the highlights of salvation history?

2. Scripture likes the image of God's people as a flock of sheep. In what specific ways does this seem an apt description? What changes might be needed if the Church were to adopt this understanding of its own identity and purpose?

3. Does God need to be persuaded to save? What's the value (or perhaps even the *point*!) in the psalmist's appeal to God to put some of His power into action on behalf of His people?

4. Notice the pronouns of the psalm—especially in the first seven verses. What is conspicuous by its absence? What conclusions might be reached on the basis of the concern of Asaph and the way that he approaches the problem?

5. Where do you hear the laughter of the Church's enemies? What can or should the Church do about this?

6. In what sense is the image of God's people as a grapevine a heightening of the point that the people are dependent on their God for everything? Which image—sheep or vine—do you find most compelling?

7. The psalmist describes the tremendous vitality and "success" of the vine as it spread and covered the land (vv. 8–11). Yet God obviously had a different vision for His chosen vine, allowing it to be pillaged by every enemy who came along. What *is* God's definition of success? How does it jibe with most of our definitions of success?

8. The psalm takes many human attributes and applies them to God. How many can your group identify? Do you think this procedure helps or hurts our understanding of God's nature and being?

9. What's the difference between calling on the Lord's (Yahweh's) name for help (v. 18) and simply looking heavenward and asking for help?

10. What is the right relationship between complete reliance on God's necessary provision (as expressed throughout the psalm and especially in v. 19), and working hard with all your might and available resources to accomplish the same thing for which you pray?

Week Five

Psalm 83

¹ O God, do not keep silence;
do not hold Your peace or be still, O God!

² For behold, Your enemies make an uproar;
those who hate You have raised their heads.

³ They lay crafty plans against Your people;
they consult together against Your treasured ones.

⁴ They say, "Come, let us wipe them out as a nation;
let the name of Israel be remembered no more!"

⁵ For they conspire with one accord;
against You they make a covenant—

⁶ the tents of Edom and the Ishmaelites,
Moab and the Hagrites,

⁷ Gebal and Ammon and Amalek,
Philistia with the inhabitants of Tyre;

⁸ Asshur also has joined them; they are the
strong arm of the children of Lot. *Selah*

⁹ Do to them as You did to Midian,
as to Sisera and Jabin at the river Kishon,

¹⁰ who were destroyed at En-dor,
who became dung for the ground.

¹¹ Make their nobles like Oreb and Zeeb,
all their princes like Zebah and Zalmunna,

¹² who said, "Let us take possession for ourselves of the pastures of God."

¹³ O my God, make them like whirling dust,
like chaff before the wind.

¹⁴ As fire consumes the forest,
as the flame sets the mountains ablaze,

¹⁵ so may You pursue them with Your tempest
and terrify them with Your hurricane!

¹⁶ Fill their faces with shame,
that they may seek Your name, O Lᴏʀᴅ.

¹⁷ Let them be put to shame and dismayed forever;
let them perish in disgrace,

¹⁸ that they may know that You alone, whose name
is the Lᴏʀᴅ, are the Most High over all the earth.

Dave Bangert

Psalm 83:1-4

> O God, do not keep silence; do not hold Your peace or be still, O God! For behold, Your enemies make an uproar; those who hate You have raised their heads. They lay crafty plans against Your people; they consult together against Your treasured ones. They say, "Come, let us wipe them out as a nation; let the name of Israel be remembered no more!"

God Will Not Keep Silent

I remember it like it was yesterday. On the first day of football practice during my senior year of high school, I hurt my knee. I would have been a starter, but instead I never got on the field until the season was half over. Then, the summer before my senior year in college, I hurt my knee again; only this time I needed surgery. About ten years after that, I hurt my knee again while coaching and had my second surgery. Then, just three weeks after finishing the therapy from that surgery, I hurt the same knee even worse and had my most serious surgery. Not finished yet, some twenty years later, I hurt that knee again and had my fourth knee surgery. It was pretty clear to me I was "cursed" when it came to knees!

It wasn't like I was blaming God, but it sure didn't seem like He was helping me out either.

My knee injuries aren't the only time I felt like I was being besieged by enemies. Despite an outward bravado, for most of my younger life I always felt like I wasn't up to par in a lot of areas. There was always, it seemed to me, someone who was better athletically, better academically, better at acting, better with the girls (okay, a lot better with the girls), better looking, and just better! I don't know that I was consumed with this comparing, but I certainly thought about it a lot. As I look back, I'm embarrassed to say that there were times I even compared myself to the apostle Paul, who felt that God had given him a "thorn" in the flesh. I figured the reason there was always someone better than me was that God had given me a "thorn." As I look back now, I can't believe how arrogant I was to think of myself like that. I'd like to blame it on youth, but in reality it was arrogance and the misguided idea that God was, as the psalmist said, keeping silent.

Somewhere at some time, I allowed my immature faith to be compromised. I allowed myself not only to feel that God was being "quiet" but also that there were enemies out to get me. I know there was many a night when I lay in bed praying for success in one area or another where I felt God was not allowing me success.

I don't really know when all those ideas of being inferior started to go away. It's not like I had all kinds of success overnight. In fact, to this day I know that there is someone more gifted than me in everything I try. But now, instead of thinking God is absent in all of this, I believe and realize that He is actually more available than ever.

I do know that, once God put a wonderful woman by the name of Jean into my life, I began to see things differently. Jean and I have been married almost twenty-nine years. During that time, I've seen, in Jean, how a humble faith that puts others first can change an attitude. Jean is the one blessing from God that made me see how utterly stupid I had been to ever think He was holding out on me. Instead of focusing on me, I began to see how faith should cause us to focus on others. The enemies that I perceived in my youth (and in my knees!) were really more attempts by Satan to cause me despair and a lack of trust in God.

As I've grown and matured in my faith, I've learned to be positive and really accept that God is in control. In many ways, this is a hard psalm for me to write about, because I rarely blame God when things go bad. To write about a psalm that is basically a "woe is me" psalm is hard!

One of the interesting parts of the beginning of this psalm is the way verse 1 is written. To me, the writer is not just asking God not to be silent; he is almost telling God. I feel like the psalmist is so confident that God will answer his plea that it is not a matter of if, but when God will come through for him. Even though God seems silent, the writer knows from past experience that God's strong, steady voice will be heard and the writer's fears will be quelled. Such a confidence can come only from a faith that is rooted in experience and trust. An experience, or perhaps many, that proved God's abiding love and ever-present concern for His children. And a trust that God's Holy Spirit continues to dwell in our lives.

You and I can share in that same confidence that the psalmist expressed. God's Spirit instills confidence in our hearts through God's Word. We have confidence that God hears us and answers us because He says so; we can ask our Father confidently in Jesus' name (John 16:23–24). Because of that, I know I can trust in God to not "keep silence." He's proven it to me over and over again.

The real key for me is to learn what Paul learned and shared in 1 Corinthians 1.

Paul says, "For the foolishness of God is wiser than men, and the weakness of God is stronger than men" (v. 25). When I was young, I seemed to measure everything according to man's strength and by man's wisdom. Now, I have learned to try to look at things from God's perspective. Yet I still fail. I still allow Satan to sow the seeds of despair. I still feel besieged at times and sometimes think God is silent. However, God *has* proven to me, through His unlimited forgiveness and love, that He will not keep silent. I know that one day I will hear His voice welcoming me to be with Him in eternity.

When I was young, I worried way too much about being popular and having a girl-friend. And, as I said, I was worried for all the wrong reasons. I thought it was all about me. God knew that and sent Jean to help me understand. Now my problem is that I don't always hear or listen to her (probably something to do with male-pattern hearing!). It can be that way with God too. When I think He's being silent, it's really a case of me not listening.

So maybe I just need to listen better. Even if I have more knee surgeries, I need to listen, because I'm confident God will be speaking to me then too. Listen to Him speak, men, even above the roaring of your enemies. He speaks to you through His Word.

....

However, God *has* proven to me, through His unlimited forgiveness and love, that He will not keep silent. I know that one day I will hear His voice welcoming me to be with Him in eternity.

Prayer: Heavenly Father, help me to tune out life's distractions and tune in to Your Word. Help me to realize that even when You seem silent, You are still working out all things for my good. In Jesus' name I pray. Amen.

....

Daily Study Questions
Psalm 83:1–4

1. A mark of wisdom, it is often claimed, is knowing when to remain silent and then doing it. How adept are you at knowing when it is one of those times when wisdom dictates silence?

2. Who is doing the talking and who is remaining silent in these verses?

3. Considering the ones making noise and the one who is silent in this text, what might we learn (or perhaps have reinforced) about the danger of talking?

4. While Israel is coping with loud enemies spouting a terrifying agenda and a God who is maddeningly silent, what, according to verse 3, is the one thing they have going for them?

5. What assurance do you have that the enemies confronting you today will not triumph over you?

Psalm 83:5–8

> For they conspire with one accord; against You they make a covenant—the tents of Edom and the Ishmaelites, Moab and the Hagrites, Gebal and Ammon and Amalek, Philistia with the inhabitants of Tyre; Asshur also has joined them; they are the strong arm of the children of Lot. *Selah*

Sufficient Grace

"Not another one!" "Come on, God; enough is enough!" "This just doesn't seem fair." "I know I said I trusted You, Lord, but how long are You going to test me?"

If you are anything like me, you've probably said those words at one time or another. Let me share a recent period in my life where it seemed that events were conspiring against me. Not too long ago, I took a call to a new position, over a thousand miles from the city my wife and I had lived for almost thirty years. We were leaving all the friends we'd made over the years, not to mention both sets of our parents. We were leaving the house where our sons had grown up; we were leaving the memories that had accumulated over the years; and we were moving to a new city where we literally didn't know anyone. Exciting? Sure it was, but also very daunting. Our confidence came from knowing it was where God was calling us to ministry. So, despite what we were leaving, we looked forward to what we were gaining. Oh, and did I mention that we hadn't sold our house before we moved, despite the fact that we had already purchased a new house in the new city? At times, it seemed like Edom and the Ishmaelites were on our tail, but we had confidence in God.

Then, on the first day I was at my new job, I found out that one of the teachers was suffering from breast cancer and would be working through that struggle. Within a week, the spouse of another teacher was diagnosed with Guillain-Barré Syndrome. It is a serious disease that, left untreated, could be with her the rest of her life. Was this Moab and the Hagrites?

But the year went on. Within two months, the economy went sour and our house still hadn't sold. Our expenses were going up as we tried to keep two houses afloat. We lowered the price. Still no takers. Was this Gebal and Ammon and Amalek?

What would come next? Another teacher had a flare-up of an existing cancer. Within two months of that, another teacher was diagnosed with skin cancer and needed a procedure for that. Just before Christmas, another teacher got the news that her father was suffering from liver cancer. He would die within six weeks of the diagnosis. Philistia and the Tyrians, perhaps?

Back in the town we had left, all four of our parents were dealing with serious health issues, including cancer and other age-related maladies. And now Asshur has joined up.

The house? It still hasn't sold, and it's been nine months on the market. Is this the straw that breaks the camel's back or is it simply the one constant that is "the strong arm of the children of Lot"?

Through this all, my wife, Jean, and I are adjusting to new jobs that God has called us to. We are adjusting to a new church home and to new friends and a new city. Six and one-half months ago, I was ready to go. Now there are days when I say, "Enough is enough!"

What really is the point of all of this? There are plenty of people who will remind you that God doesn't give us more than we can handle. But, most of the time, that doesn't provide a lot of comfort, does it? Things don't always get better; sometimes they get worse. Sometimes things just keep getting added on. I'm pretty sure that's where Asaph was at. He was trying to tell God that the situation was worse than it had ever been. He was saying that, no matter where Israel turned, there was a threat. I've felt that way recently as I struggle not to let the laundry list of impediments to doing God's work overwhelm me.

To me, the key in handling these situations is in remembering that it isn't a bunch of different things attacking my faith in God. It is one being—Satan. He takes my sin and the sins of the world around me and turns them against my faith. He is the one who seeks to grind out a victory over my confidence in God. Just as it seemed there was an array of countries lined up against Israel, so it seems like there is an array of disappointments and ailments lined up against me.

Honestly, I don't think I can handle this. In fact, I know I can't. That is why I too take my list of fears to God. I bring my Hagrites and Tyrians and Amalekites to God. I'll let Him handle it. God knows how, and He has the power to do it.

When I got to my new school, they already had a verse picked out for the year's theme. It was 2 Corinthians 12:9–10: "But He said to me, 'My grace is sufficient for you, for My power is made perfect in weakness.' Therefore I will boast all the more gladly of my weaknesses, so that the power of Christ may rest upon me. For the sake of Christ, then, I am content with weaknesses, insults, hardships, persecutions, and calamities. For when

I am weak, then I am strong."

I can't tell you how many times I've turned to these words. You see, sometimes it's not just a matter of faith that gets you through tough times. Sometimes—no, really all the time—it is a matter of knowing what you can't handle. These situations are things I can't handle. The real joy and peace comes in knowing in faith that I don't have to. That's right, I don't have to. That's what God's love is all about. It's about Him loving me so much that He forgives me when I try to handle "stuff" on my own. He forgives me when I think I am the source of the power, when it is really a gift from God through His Holy Spirit. He surrounds me with His protecting love when the "strong arm of the children of Lot" gets a little too threatening. And, above all, He assures me through His Word and Sacrament that all of this love and forgiveness and protection will never end.

I'd like to tell you that everyone in this story is fine now. I'd like to tell you that the house has sold. But I can't. I'd like to tell you that I don't worry. I'd like to tell you that I never have moments of lost confidence. I'd like to tell you that I never doubt God. But I can't. I can tell you that, more than ever, I know my weaknesses. I also know, more than ever, that God's power is more than enough to make up for my weaknesses. His grace *is* enough—even when the Ishmaelites and Moabites and Ammonites are at the door to my heart. Praise be to God for His love and grace through our Savior, Jesus Christ!

....

These situations are things I can't handle. The real joy and peace comes in knowing in faith that I don't have to. That's right, I don't have to. That's what God's love is all about.

Prayer: Dear God, You know that there are things in my life that I can't handle. Take away my foolish pride and strengthen my confidence and trust in You. Your grace is sufficient, and for it I am grateful. In Jesus' name. Amen.

....

1. What are the names of the threatening forces that lately seem to be ganging up on you?

2. In what sense is it right to see these as spiritual threats that challenge your faith?

3. What would have motivated all of the surrounding nations to conspire against Israel?

4. Why would it be fair to conclude that Israel is not the real target of the surrounding nations' hatred?

5. How will recognition of the spiritual component of the coming day's challenges affect how you deal with them?

Psalm 83:9-12

> Do to them as you did to Midian, as to Sisera and Jabin at the river Kishon, who were destroyed at En-dor, who became dung for the ground. Make their nobles like Oreb and Zeeb, all their princes like Zebah and Zalmunna, who said, "Let us take possession for ourselves of the pastures of God."

Enemies—Defeated

Most of my life, I have been involved in athletics, either as a team member, fan, or coach. Most of the time, I disliked some opposing teams so much that it would be fair to say that I really hated losing to them more than other teams. It also gave me more than the usual amount of joy to defeat those teams.

I think of being in high school and absolutely despising anything that had to do with our sister school, which was nicknamed the Red Knights. I had a football coach who absolutely forbade us to lose to them. Later on, I had the opportunity to coach against the Red Knights and it was the game of the year, no matter what the records said. In high school, I despised the very sight of a Red Knight letter jacket or anything that was remotely related to "them." Of course, the irony of the situation is that I ended up marrying a "Red Knight" and, by extension, into an entire family of Red Knights.

Blessed by a number of good athletes when I was coaching high school girls' basketball, my team won five conference championships in ten years. The other five years, we finished either second or third. Our main competition was the Pacers from another Lutheran school. Our rivalry was both intense and respectful, yet there was no one I wanted to beat more, no one I wanted to see lose more, than them.

Growing up in Wisconsin, I was bred to "hate" anything about Illinois teams. The Bears, the Cubs, the Illini—I want to see all of them lose—with regularity! Even now that I've moved to Texas, I still follow "my" teams with special notice when they play those rivals that I've come to hate.

Yes, I know, I used the word *hate*. We're not really supposed to hate anyone, are we? Yet, in the emotional world of athletics—and perhaps even rivalries of any type, we do feel emotions that get close to hate. Perhaps we've even found ourselves perilously close to the precipice where we ask God to be on our side against our rivals. Whether correct or not, I have prayed before many a game for a win—a victory over my enemy on the playing field or in the arena. I want God on *my* side.

In Psalm 83, Asaph is asking God to destroy all of Israel's enemies. Israel was fighting for its survival and was tired of getting beat up. They hated these countries, and not just because they lost a game once in a while. These countries represented values systems and religions that threatened Israel, God's people. These countries represented, in very real ways, death and slavery to the people of Israel. And Asaph doesn't want just God's help; he wants God to turn them into "dung" (worm food; v. 10) as He's done before. Almost like an old coach ruminating on victories past, the psalmist conjures up names of great Godvictories of the past (Midian, Sisera, Jabin).

So, two main lessons really come to my mind here. One is how I have a tendency to make big issues out of things that aren't really that big of a deal. When I worry about winning games or getting ahead in life or some petty rivalry I have with someone, I may pray for God to be on my side. Yet the reality is that those aren't issues at all when compared to the spiritual warfare that goes on in my life and the lives of those around me. When the psalmist called out to God, he was concerned about the very existence of Israel as God's people. Is spiritual existence my concern when I call out to God? Not often enough, I fear. My perceived "need" for God is almost always something personal. The idea of being wiped out spiritually doesn't occur to me very often. Perhaps I am overconfident. Any good coach will tell you that overconfidence leads to upsets. Is my complacency a cause for concern? It should, at the very least, propel me to evaluate anew where my priorities lie when I pray to God to be on my side.

Second, I think of the whole concept of God being "on my side." It reminds me of Joshua before the battle for Jericho. In Joshua 5, a conversation between Joshua and the messenger of God takes place: "When Joshua was by Jericho, he lifted up his eyes and looked, and behold, a man was standing before him with his drawn sword in his hand. And Joshua went to him and said to him, 'Are you for us, or for our adversaries?' And he said, 'No; but I am the commander of the army of the Lord. Now I have come'" (vv. 13–14). You would think that if God was ever going to acknowledge which side He was on, it would be with Joshua. Joshua was a new commander, and the confidence that would have come with knowing God was on his side would have done wonders. So maybe it is the question that is wrong.

Perhaps the question we need to ask ourselves is not "is God on my side" but "Am I on God's side?" Am I reviewing my life choices through the lenses of God's role in my life or am I simply looking for God to give me an easy way out? In God's Word, we have His blueprint for our life in many places. It is not hard to find an outline for the Christian life God desires for us. Through His grace and by the power of His Spirit, God enables us to "be on His side," to follow the blueprint. Through faith in Christ, we are aligned with God and are on His side.

In the end, our first prayer should always be for the courage, strength, and power to stay in the faith. As God, in His grace, grants us that request, we are able to put the issues of life in perspective. Our rivals, our enemies, are nothing compared to the enemies that threaten our faith and relationship to God. Making sure we align ourselves with God's will and Word is eternally more important than worrying about whether we'll beat the Red Knights.

....

Through His grace and by the power of His Spirit, God enables us to "be on His side," to follow the blueprint. Through faith in Christ, we are aligned with God and are on His side.

Prayer: Lord Jesus Christ, You defeated my chief enemies—sin, Satan, and death—by death on the cross. Help me in my life to bring honor to You and Your Father, who with the Holy Spirit are one God, now and forever. Amen.

....

1. What's the most intense rivalry in which you have been a personal participant?

2. How did (do!) you feel about your rivals? Were those feelings justified or even fair?

3. When Asaph recalls Israel's historic rivals, is he describing simple rivalries such as those that exist between small-town football teams or between dog owners and cat caretakers, or is there something more at stake than mere preference or tribalism?

4. How do you distinguish between mere rivals and real enemies?

5. What rivals and what enemies need your prayers right now?

Psalm 83:13–16

O my God, make them like whirling dust, like chaff before the wind. As fire consumes the forest, as the flame sets the mountains ablaze, so may You pursue them with Your tempest and terrify them with Your hurricane! Fill their faces with shame, that they may seek Your name, O LORD.

You Alone

Rrinnggg . . . It was a strange time for the phone to ring. It was a school night, around 9:00 p.m. Our sons, about 4 and 2 at the time, were already in bed. I picked up: "Hello." "Uh, Mr. Bangert, it's me." I knew exactly who it was. Lisa (not her real name) was in the junior theology class I taught. She liked to come and talk to me. She showed some signs of depression, but didn't seem to be much worse than a lot of other kids. "Hi, Lisa; why are you calling?" "I did something pretty stupid." "That's okay; we all do stupid things, Lisa. Do you want to tell me about it?" "Well, I guess. I guess I kind of, you know, cut my wrists." My mind jumped into overdrive. What do I do? Whom do I call? How do I fix this situation? How can I solve this situation, take care of Lisa's problems, and be the great fixer on the white horse who comes riding in at the last minute?

"Excuse me, Mr. Bangert; can I talk to you a minute?" It was Erik (again, not his real name). He was a senior, one of the students I was assigned to as counselor at the high school where I worked. He was a smaller kid but a nice guy. We had talked about college stuff before and the fact that he and his parents weren't getting along real well. "Sure, come on in," I said. I figured it would be another routine chat. "Can I close the door?" "Sure," I said, knowing that, when a student asked to close the door, it was generally anything but routine. "You're the only person I can think of to tell this to. I hope you don't mind. But I have to tell someone," Eric continued on. And then he really continued: "You see, Mr. B, I'm gay." Again, my mind started to race. Whom do I have to tell? Will he get kicked out of school? But I believe God still loves him. Every kid in this school is going to know; he'll be taunted. But I need to tell him this lifestyle is wrong. How do I solve this, fix Erik's problems, and be the great fixer on the white horse?

This time the phone call came at 2:00 a.m. on the Friday night before graduation.

It was our valedictorian on the phone. "Mr. Bangert, I can't sleep. I—we—did something stupid to a teacher's house. He caught us and I'm not sure if he knows it was me. The guilt is killing me and my parents will kill me if I can't be valedictorian. What do I do?" Here we go again, I thought. How do I save this kid from this problem? How do I solve this?

There was also the time my wife and I came home from our younger son's freshman football game to an empty garage and a house with lots of lights on. That seems strange, we both said. When we walked in the house, one look at our older son said it all—something was wrong. "Dad, I was in an accident and the car is really bad." "Was anyone hurt?" was the first question out of my mouth, and when the answer was "no," I just hugged him and let him get the fear out of his system. I wanted to be the dad who makes everything better, who fixes all the problems, and makes the bad stuff disappear.

These are just a few examples from my life, but I'm sure you have a few of your own. You know what I mean, those times in life where we want to be the fixer [another devotion writer mentioned this earlier]. We think we should be able to take care of all the problems. Especially as a man, a husband, a dad, we're supposed to be the hero who rides in on the white horse and takes care of it all. Sometimes we do, or at least we think we do, only to see things fall apart again, somewhere else or maybe the same problem all over again. It takes us a while to realize we aren't the hero on the white horse. Sometimes that just depresses us and other times it causes us to go for help.

I think Asaph, in verses 13–16, may have been at that point. He was frustrated that Israel's enemies kept coming and that he (the writer) and they (the Israelites) couldn't fix the situation. They needed someone on a white horse to ride in and save the day. So he called on God. He didn't just ask for a little help; no, he was very direct. "O my God, make them like whirling dust," "pursue them with Your tempest," "terrify them with Your hurricane," and "fill their faces with shame" are a few of the terms he used when asking God for help. I'll give the palmist some credit; when he asked God for help, he certainly asked God to go all the way!

I don't know about you, but when I'm confronted with a problem, I try to handle things on my own first. I'm sure my solutions to the problems above would have been better and clearer if I, and they, had gone to God right away. You see, I don't know about you, but I don't look anything like a knight on a white horse. I don't even know how to ride a horse, much less go into battle on one. But God does. It is to Him we need to turn, immediately. In fact, in Revelation 19:11, we read, "Then I saw heaven opened, and behold, a white horse! The one sitting on it is called Faithful and True, and in righteousness He judges and makes war." The reference is most probably to Christ as the Messiah King. He is the person on the white horse who rides in to save the day—*our day*!

When we want justice, when we want things to be okay, God is our only hope. It was Christ who, in that room the evening after His resurrection, knew the perfect word to utter to a group of scared disciples: "Peace." That is the only word we need to hear. It renders worthless all of our "manly" human attempts to fix things. His peace, love, and forgiveness is the ultimate answer to making things better.

Lisa recovered and graduated. Erik did get a lot of taunting. But he and I spent a lot of time in Scripture together and he got some counseling from his pastor. He, too, graduated and weathered the storm. The valedictorian apologized to the teacher, gave the speech, and now is a very successful writer. My son learned some lessons that night, one of which, I hope, was that we loved him a lot and would stand by him. And Asaph? He got his answer too. The one we all got. God is there to help us out. He proved it by sending His Son to handle the biggest problem of all!

....

In that room the evening after His resurrection, [Christ] knew the perfect word to utter to a group of scared disciples: "Peace." That is the only word we need to hear.

Prayer: Dear Lord, help me to keep the responsibilities and vocations that You have given me in perspective. Thank You for sending me Your Son, my Savior, Jesus Christ. In His name I pray. Amen.

....

1. When was a time that you tried the "knight in shining armor" routine, only to watch helplessly as your efforts came to naught or actually exacerbated the situation?

2. How does a man know when it is time to give it his all and when it is time to give it up and appeal to God?

3. What does the psalmist teach us about the relationship between God and His creation?

4. What difference does a richer understanding of God's actions in and through nature make for the way we think about "natural disasters"?

5. The psalmist prays for severe judgment, that is true; but what does he hope will result from this divine judgment against God's enemies?

Psalm 83:17–18

> Let them be put to shame and dismayed forever; let them perish in disgrace, that they may know that You alone, whose name is the LORD, are the Most High over all the earth.

God Most High

Just before I sat down at my computer to write this devotion, I checked an on-line news service. The top three stores all had to do with senseless killings. A man drives through two southern towns and kills at least nine people (most of them strangers), a student in another country kills fifteen people, and a parishioner walks into church and kills the pastor while shooting up the church. As I read the stories, a few facts really stood out in my mind. One was that authorities said that, in all three cases, the shooter had many more guns and ammunition available and could have, conceivably, killed many more. Second, in all the cases, the authorities were trying to find out why the senseless killings took place. Finally, one of the law-enforcement people in the incident in the South said something to the effect that it was one of the worst scenes he had ever seen. There were others?

Unfortunately, we see atrocities like this on the news far too often. At times, we become immune; at other times, there may be some segment of the story that seems to really connect with us. In the incident in the South, one of the deputies involved in the chase found out that his wife and child were two of the innocent victims. Moments like that tend to elicit a stronger reaction from people who question God's involvement and God's decision making. At some point, we are forced to deal with the grim realities of a world filled with sin.

Our world *is* filled with sin and its consequences; we see this at every turn. Yet it is often hard for people of God to understand what type of desperation or hatred could drive people to randomly kill others. The psalmist may have asked the same question as he felt the oppression of Israel all around him. Would it never end? Would their enemies never stop? What kind of hatred drives Israel's enemies to the never-ending attacks? Those feelings may be what drove Asaph, in desperation, to call out for God's vengeance to be meted out upon Israel's enemies. Yet, in the end, he gives us a verse that hints at who this God is. Verse 18 says "That they may know that You alone, whose name is the LORD, are the Most High over all the earth." Here the psalmist invokes God's gracious, covenantal name, Yahweh, to describe the Most High. God is just, and He will crush His enemies and the enemies of His people. But God is also a God of love, and He will save.

When I'm upset with things that I want God to take care of, my motive is usually very personal. I want things my way because I think I have been persecuted in some way and deserve something from God. After all, I surmise, I think I've been a pretty good guy and have always tried to do what God wants; so what if my motive is a lot less noble than that of Asaph's? I only want what's fair . . . in my own individual world.

My emotions probably run the way this psalm runs. First, I get tired of all the crummy stuff in my life and I want to clean it up. So I pray and pray and ask and plead for God to change things to my way. At some point, I probably try to make a deal with God that if He does something then I'll reciprocate. Then, most times, my sin of selfishness is pointed out and I realize that God's love is for all people and being fair isn't part of the deal. What I know I should be praying for is that God's love is made clear to all the people who are trying to deal with the sin and hatred that is eating way at their individual lives. Even more so, I should concentrate on sharing the Good News ahead of time so that, perhaps by the power and influence of God, some of the sin doesn't happen.

Years ago, at one of my former schools, a new freshman student did not list a home church on his school forms. I also remember, very clearly, that he still didn't list one as a senior. That really bothered me then and it still bothers me now. Most church-related schools, like ours, proclaim evangelism as part of their mission. And I have seen many students and families come to the Lord because of the words and concern from a school. But in this case, I think we may have failed. To this day, it still haunts me that I was part of that failure. In all the times I met with that student, I'm not sure I engaged him in a discussion about his faith. He was a good kid, fairly innocuous in most ways, so no one bothered him—even when we should have.

I bring this up now because I was reminded of it by verses 17–18. Did we leave that student to be ashamed and dismayed? Will he perish in disgrace? Will I see him in heaven? Obviously, I don't know the answers to these questions. I can only trust in God's mercy and in His promise that He will save all those He has predestined to eternal life. What I do know is that not confronting that student was easier for me. Being passive with him was another example of satisfying *my* need for *my* life to be easy.

In Philippians, we hear Paul say, "Therefore God has highly exalted Him and bestowed on him the name that is above every name, so that at the name of Jesus every knee should bow, in heaven and on earth and under the earth, and every tongue confess that Jesus Christ is Lord, to the glory of God the Father" (2:9–11). That verse really brings it all together for me. It helps point out why God sent Jesus and helps me understand Psalm 83 too.

On the surface, Psalm 83, seemed to me to be all about destruction and having God avenge the times we feel wronged. Yet, as I got closer to the end, I felt this psalm leading me in a different direction. I needed to go back to the crucified and resurrected Christ, who died to put away the guilt of our sin. I needed to understand that while God exacts justice for His people, He also wants people to turn to Him in repentant faith to escape His wrath. The Most High, the sovereign God of the universe, also is God who loves us dearly.

This psalm also reminded me that I need to spend more time with people like that young graduate. I need to tell them why God sent His Son, Jesus, and why, at some point, we *all* will confess that Jesus is Lord.

I'm sure we'll read more news reports that bother us. But let us take solitude in the fact that we have "A Mighty Fortress" on our side. A God who is the Most High and, by the power of the Holy Spirit, reigns in our lives now and in eternity forever.

....

I needed to understand that while God exacts justice for His people, He also wants people to turn to Him in repentant faith to escape His wrath. The Most High, the sovereign God of the universe, also is God who loves us dearly.

Prayer: Dear Holy Spirit, when I'm confronted by bad news about the world around me, comfort me with Your presence. Give me the courage to do the right thing, trusting in the merits of my Savior. I ask this in Jesus' name. Amen.

....

Daily Study Questions
Psalm 83:17–18

1. What circumstances or wrongs are most likely to awaken in you a demand for justice or even vengeance?

2. Is the psalmist's prayer motivated by a desire for vengeance or by something else?

3. What difference is there between acknowledging God's reign as sovereign Creator and Lord of all, and confessing Him as one's Savior and God?

4. How does verse 18 challenge the widely held notion that all religions actually worship the same God?

5. What difference should it make for you to remember that God is not a regional deity or a patron lord of a particular people, but the "Most High over *all the earth*"?

Week Five

Psalm 83

The 83rd psalm is a psalm of prayer. It is much the same as Psalm 80, which clearly spells out the names of the Gentile nations; therefore, the same summary applies.

-Martin Luther

Week Five, Psalm 83
GROUP BIBLE STUDY
(Questions and answers are on pp. 210-13.)

1. Describe a time in your life (maybe from childhood or perhaps just recently) when you had to deal with a bully. How did you handle it? How did it turn out?

2. Asaph is quite specific and perhaps even abrupt in his appeal (some might say demand) for God to do something about the loud and dangerous enemies who are threatening His people. How does this prayer fit with the typical prayer, "if it be Your will," so regularly heard today? Would Asaph's prayer be better if it included the phrase "according to God's will"?

3. Millennia old, the evil intent voiced in verse four sounds thoroughly and eerily contemporary. Does this verse serve only to highlight the rabid anti-Semitism that has been a sad (indeed, too often horrific) and recurrent theme in world history, or might a more considered interpretation of the verse contain even richer and more relevant spiritual truth?

4. The psalmist's list of tribes and peoples that were arrayed against Israel reads like a veritable rogues gallery of ancient Fertile-Crescent bullies. Why was this threat about more than politics?

5. Is Asaph simply suffering from a persecution complex? Is there a reason for Christians today to be concerned about the threats that encompass them, or would that be succumbing to unfounded paranoia?

OKAY TO COPY THIS PAGE.   146

6. When Asaph considers the threats that surround Israel, he prays for the kind of intervention that had brought low Israel's enemies in centuries long past. How does the recollection of old victories bring comfort in the present? What are some old memories you can use to bring you encouragement during new trials?

7. Consider the psalmist's chosen examples of Israel's past victories (Judges 4 and 7–8). What do these two stories have in common? What point does the psalmist make by choosing these stories?

8. How does the imprecatory prayer of Asaph (longing to see his neighbors reduced to dung; v. 10) square with our Lord's command to love our enemies (Matthew 5:43–47)?

9. In verse 17, Asaph drives home the sharp point of his prayer for the Lord's wrath to be unleashed on Israel's enemies, pleading that they may "be put to shame and dismayed forever . . . [to] perish in disgrace." Yet, in the very next verse, he indicates that he offers this harsh petition only as a means to his final desire: that these enemies "may know that You alone . . . are the Most High." How can those who perish know the Lord? How might you reconcile these two verses?

10. How will your increased understanding of the spiritual war being waged on the battleground called earth shape the way that you think, act, speak, and pray in the coming week? What do those around you need from you if you are faithfully to witness God's truth about this spiritual conflict?

Week Six

Psalm 90

1 Lord, You have been our dwelling place in all generations.

2 Before the mountains were brought forth,
or ever You had formed the earth and the world,
from everlasting to everlasting You are God.

3 You return man to dust and say,
"Return, O children of man!"

4 For a thousand years in Your sight are but as yesterday when it is past, or as a watch in the night.

5 You sweep them away as with a flood; they are like
a dream, like grass that is renewed in the morning:

6 in the morning it flourishes and is renewed;
in the evening it fades and withers.

7 For we are brought to an end by Your anger;
by Your wrath we are dismayed.

8 You have set our iniquities before You,
our secret sins in the light of Your presence.

9 For all our days pass away under Your wrath;
we bring our years to an end like a sigh.

10 The years of our life are seventy, or even by reason of strength eighty; yet their span is but toil and
trouble; they are soon gone, and we fly away.

[11] Who considers the power of Your anger,
and Your wrath according to the fear of You?

[12] So teach us to number our days
that we may get a heart of wisdom.

[13] Return, O Lord! How long? Have pity on Your servants!

[14] Satisfy us in the morning with Your steadfast love,
that we may rejoice and be glad all our days.

[15] Make us glad for as many days as You have afflicted us,
and for as many years as we have seen evil.

[16] Let Your work be shown to your servants,
and Your glorious power to their children.

[17] Let the favor of the Lord our God be upon us,
and establish the work of our hands upon us;
yes, establish the work of our hands!

Frank Fischer

Psalm 90:1–2

> Lord, You have been our dwelling place in all generations. Before the mountains were brought forth, or ever You had formed the earth and the world, from everlasting to everlasting You are God.

Our Dwelling Place

Have you ever paused to look at the stars in a remote open space, or even in your yard during a still night, and took in the silent serenity and vastness of the universe? Or maybe instead of looking up, you have flown in an airplane over the expansive world beneath you, observing all the ant-sized people scurrying about their busy lives. Seeing such a sight, maybe you even wondered where everyone was going in such a hurry. Then perhaps the captain's announcing the aircraft's descent shook you from your contemplation of the world below just as you were about to reenter the busyness of your own life.

It is so hard for us mere mortals to get our minds around what it really means to belong to an eternal God. God is our "dwelling place," Moses says; God is "from everlasting to everlasting." Because the pace of our contemporary lives is intense, if not overwhelming, sometimes we lose that insight. Advertisements, e-mails, texts, IMs, and calls hunt us down no matter where we are, all vying for our attention. The majesty, power, and eternal nature of our God—and our own mortality—can get lost in the thick whirlwind of our hurried existence.

There's an old saying, "When you are surrounded by alligators, don't forget that your objective is to drain the swamp." Keeping our earthly existence in perspective and staying focused on eternity is a real challenge. And yet, we should remember that our God created us and all things. He knows we need to earn a living, rear our children, and keep pace with the demands that are placed on us. Our Christian beliefs are not just something that we mutter on Sunday mornings. God's love and grace in Christ, and the Spirit's presence, are real, and they impact us in our daily lives. The Gospel of God's Son is powerful. Paul even says that "the word of the cross. . . is the power of God" (1 Corinthians 1:18). With our Lord forgiving and daily guiding us through His Word, we can trust Him to help us in all we do. With His help, we can do His work and meet our obligations.

This does not come naturally to us. Martin Luther stated that we are in a constant struggle with the devil, the world, and our own sinful flesh. So how do we overcome these obstacles? Apart from Christ, we can't. But in Christ, God gives us all that we need. Through the Gospel of His Son, Jesus Christ, God forgives, uplifts, and sustains us. Jesus is our source of forgiveness and strength. Transformed by God's grace, which we receive through faith, we can begin to work God's way. What are some good ways to remember what is eternally important?

First, we can begin each day with prayer. The Lord has promised to hear our prayers for the sake of Christ. We pray in repentant faith, trusting the Holy Spirit to guide us as we petition the Lord, asking Him to hear us and answer according to His will. Unlike some requests that God may deny, a prayer for stronger faith and spiritual fortitude is something God always desires for us. In 1 Thessalonians 5: 16–18, Paul tells us, "Rejoice always, pray without ceasing, give thanks in all circumstances; for this is the will of God in Christ Jesus for you." We can ask God to give us joy and hearts filled with thankful prayer.

I begin most days with prayer, oftentimes in the shower or as I have breakfast. I do not always take a lengthy period of time to pray, but there are short periods where I can focus on talking with God. Prayer does not have to be limited to kneeling down and reciting a memorized prayer or reading one out of a book (although there's a written prayer at the end of this devotion); prayer can also be extemporaneous. It is a time for you to be yourself with your Creator. He knows your heart and He sees how you interface with everyone else, so why would interfacing with Him be any different?

You can pray anywhere: in your car on the way to or from work (and not just after a near-miss), during a break in your day, before a meal, and before going to bed. What about in public? Whether in the cafeteria or a restaurant, pausing briefly to give thanks is the right thing to do. I know it can be uncomfortable to stop for prayer in a public place, especially when you are with business associates, but even this can be a witness to our God. When I first started to pray publicly, I was very uncomfortable, almost embarrassed. I only did so when I was alone. Over time, it became more natural for me. I do not generally fold my hands in an obvious manner. I just take a moment to close my eyes, bow my head slightly, and mentally thank God for His blessings, 15 to 20 seconds at most. I don't try to be obvious or overtly pious and, to be honest, I'm still working on the courage to offer a prayer with business associates.

Besides prayer, I use visual reminders to help me keep Christ out front. We are His ambassadors to this world during every step of every day, not just during Christian events. For example, I have Christian affirmations on my dresser and my desk at work. They are both small 365-page daily calendars with a Bible verse or a Christian-themed quote. I flip to a new day and read it each morning as I leave my bedroom or arrive at my desk. Oftentimes, the verse somehow relates directly to an issue I am struggling with or something I encounter during the day.

Another visual reminder, which I also see in many other cars, is a cross hanging from the rearview mirror. Every time I drive, I remember my Christian roots—and it curbs my hand gestures and use of expletives when some "Bozo" cuts me off. Some people put Christian bumper stickers or symbols on their cars to witness their faith. Even that gets my attention and helps my focus. I also keep a miniature portrait of the head of Christ in my wallet. Every time I open it up, Jesus in the picture is looking back at me. Growing up, my dad and I had never discussed our faith. But early on when I was in high school, I noticed he had a picture of our Lord in his wallet, and that really hit me. I guess that's what prompted me to follow suit at some point later. I hope I have that same impact on my son.

A few years back, our pastor challenged the members of our congregation to each develop a personal mission statement. It was in the context of this very subject: The Lord is our dwelling place throughout all generations. My personal mission statement is "To aggressively, not passively, provide Christ-centered leadership in all areas of my life, in support of my family, friends, and Christian ministries, while maintaining a balanced commitment to those who depend on me." I keep it on my desk. Every so often, I reflect on whether my objectives and activities are in keeping with my defined mission. If not, a good kick is in order. Perhaps a personal mission statement is something you might consider.

We all think and process information differently. Perhaps visual reminders would not work for you. But I encourage you to do something to keep your Lord and your faith an active part of your daily chaos. Please do not just compartmentalize your faith as something useful only on Sundays. Find ways to allow your faith to infiltrate everything you do in every part of your life. The Lord is also your dwelling place, your place of security and refuge not only in this life but also in the life of the world to come.

God gives us all that we need. Through the
Gospel of His Son, Jesus Christ, God forgives,
uplifts, and sustains us. Jesus is our source of
forgiveness and strength.

Prayer: Heavenly Father, You are my dwelling place. From eternity, You have called me to be Your son through the Gospel. Throughout the day, guide my steps and remind me of Your unfailing love. I ask this through Jesus, my Lord. Amen.

Monday

Daily Study Questions
Psalm 90:1–2

1. What's the longest you've lived in one place? What are the benefits of living long in one place?

2. How does one have God for a dwelling place? What would it mean to dwell in God?

3. Does verse 1 communicate a message of hope and comfort, or one of rebuke and warning? How does the second verse support your conclusions?

4. Why do you think Moses, the author of this psalm, makes the comparison between God and His creation?

5. In the coming day, how can you cultivate a greater awareness of God as your dwelling place?

Psalm 90:3-6

You return man to dust and say, "Return, O children of man!" For a thousand years in Your sight are but as yesterday when it is past, or as a watch in the night. You sweep them away as with a flood; they are like a dream, like grass that is renewed in the morning: in the morning it flourishes and is renewed; in the evening it fades and withers.

From Dust . . . to Heaven

On March 2, 2009, a two-month-old baby passed away in her crib from Sudden Infant Death Syndrome. On March 8, a Christian pastor was preaching his sermon in a church 20 miles northeast of St. Louis when a deranged gunman entered the sanctuary and shot the 45-year-old man of God to death. On March 12, a 95-year-old Christian nurse died quietly in her sleep. Death is everywhere, and none can escape it. Most people leave this earth by natural causes, some through violence, and others from disease, but no one is immune.

Death and suffering are inevitable. No one likes to talk about it, think about it, or face it. Yet death is just another result of our sin. God has every right to be angry and vengeful with us. In the previous study, we discussed the fact that we belong to God, that He is our dwelling place. Yet we often fail to recognize or acknowledge that relationship, and we most certainly sin every day. Can you imagine how frustrated and disappointed (though not surprised) He must have been? He created us as perfect, holy, and righteous creatures, in His image, intending for us to live peacefully and eternally with Him. Then we blew it in the Garden and fell from that relationship. Thank God that He sent Jesus to restore us to Himself.

Think about the last time someone you love or relied on disappointed you. Perhaps it was a parent who promised to take you to a ball game but didn't. Perhaps it was a friend or co-worker who committed to do something but blew you off. Perhaps it was a spouse who was unfaithful. Perhaps it was a child who ignored his or her upbringing and followed a path of destruction. I remember how disappointed I was when my then 21-year-old daughter decided to move in with her boyfriend of two years. We discussed my viewpoint and expectations; we discussed the biblical perspective; but in the end, she moved in with him anyway. I still loved and supported her, and we saw each other every week, but she always knew where I stood regarding her living arrangements. Five years later, they married and are now living a fulfilled life. As much as I was disappointed, I too am a sinner and have many faults of my own. How much more then would God be disappointed, and disgusted, with our choices, given that He is holy and perfect?

But we must endure the pain and agony of this life only for a short time, relatively speaking anyway. It's funny how in different circumstances, time seems to pass at different rates. When I'm doing something that I enjoy and get totally absorbed into, time flies by very quickly—like a riveting movie, a good book, or woodworking project. Yet when I sit in a dentist chair (no offense to the dentists out there) or find myself doing something that I'd rather not be doing, time drags on forever.

The reading for today states that to God, a thousand years are like a day or a night watch. While we cannot truly comprehend eternity, our seventy to eighty years on this earth are very short when put in the context of eternity. It seems a long time while we live it, like being in the dentist chair, but in the grand scheme of things, it is short. When as children we were put in the corner for being bad, sitting there seemed like forever, all five minutes worth. But afterward we moved on to happier activities. So it is with life on earth. We must suffer for five minutes—over 80 years—before moving on to the activities God has in store for us eternally. Our lives are nothing more than a hash mark on the continuum of eternity. In 1 Corinthians 15:42–49, God describes His take on things:

> So is it with the resurrection of the dead. What is sown is perishable; what is raised is imperishable. It is sown in dishonor; it is raised in glory. It is sown in weakness; it is raised in power. It is sown a natural body; it is raised a spiritual body. If there is a natural body, there is also a spiritual body. Thus it is written, "The first man Adam became a living being"; the last Adam became a life-giving spirit. But it is not the spiritual that is first but the natural, and then the spiritual. The first man was from the earth, a man of dust; the second man is from heaven. As was the man of dust, so also are those who are of the dust, and as is the man of heaven, so also are those who are of heaven. Just as we have borne the image of the man of dust, we shall also bear the image of the man of heaven.

God's anger with us is warranted. He sentenced us to death, both physically and spiritually. We were subject to His divine wrath and eternal damnation. But He also loves us, and proved that unequivocally by sending His own Son to live, suffer, die, and be raised again for us as a human being, just like us, although without sin. We are only asked to suffer for a short time, and He has provided redemption for us out of grace through faith in Christ Jesus. We even have brief periods of joy and peace while living our lives. For those who believe, He has promised to hear us and answer our prayers in a way that is best for us and His kingdom on earth. Just as the children of Israel wandered in the desert for forty years before coming to the Promised Land, so is our sojourn on earth until reaching our undeserved, heavenly home for eternity. Praise be to God, who satisfied His own divine requirement for justice by sending us Jesus, so that we escape the punishment we deserve and instead attain eternity with Him.

....

God's anger with us is warranted . . . We were subject to His divine wrath and eternal damnation. But He also loves us, and proved that unequivocally by sending His own Son.

Prayer: Lord Jesus, I am made of dust and will one day return to dust. Forgive me, Lord, and restore God's image in me, so that I may live to serve You and the people You have put in my life here on earth, so that more people may attain heaven. I ask this in Your name. Amen.

....

Tuesday

Daily Study Questions
Psalm 90:3–6

1. What biblical story comes to mind when you read the words "dust" and "return" in verse 3?

2. In verse 3, what reason is given for man's death? Is it "natural causes"?

3. A thousand years is for God little more than a day or a four-hour division of the night. Does this fact comfort you or terrify you?

4. Why is the image of a surging flood that obliterates everything in its path (v. 5a) an accurate and potent picture of human existence?

5. How should these rather bleak verses about the sad facts of human life affect the way that you live the coming day?

Psalm 90:7-10

For we are brought to an end by Your anger; by Your wrath we are dismayed. You have set our iniquities before You, our secret sins in the light of Your presence. For all our days pass away under Your wrath; we bring our years to an end like a sigh. The years of our life are seventy, or even by reason of strength eighty; yet their span is but toil and trouble; they are soon gone, and we fly away.

God Remains Faithful

Imagine having someone you like and trust turn on you so fiercely that initially it is incomprehensible. In 1990, I started a new job at a new company. I was one of three directors forming a start-up division. We were a team of peers with different responsibilities. About three months into the job, the other two directors were demoted to managers reporting to me. I was not informed about this organizational change until minutes before it was announced. The two peers accused me of orchestrating the change. One person resigned immediately, with class and dignity. The other stayed and seemed to support me to my face while undermining me to customers, subordinates, and other management. This went on for months, at first without my knowledge, then while I tried to restore the relationship, and finally while I documented events to conclusively prove the insubordination. I really liked and trusted this person implicitly. I was totally mortified and crushed by this incident.

Now multiply my experience times several billion people over thousands of years, and it won't even come close to the righteous anger God has for sin. In the previous study, we established that our earthly lives are really just brief moments in the continuum of eternity. The wages of sin is death but, because of Jesus, believers are assured of eternal life in perfect, resurrected bodies in a new heaven and earth. But what about the content of those moments—our lives? These verses in Psalm 90 reflect the significance of sin and the reasons that life is so hard. We brought these things on ourselves. God allows life to be difficult as punishment for man's disobedience.

Take a moment to reflect on your behaviors from the last week. Can you identify the things that would condemn you? God recounts them and puts them before Himself. Not a pretty picture at all. If you think about it, they fall into many categories. There are the big, obvious ones: lying, stealing, lust, profanity, hand gestures, compulsions, (worse?), and so on. Then there are the more subtle ones: inappropriate jokes, speeding, misleading someone, verbal abuse, omission, and so on. But the last category might not even enter our minds: unjust criticism, arrogance, insensitivity, eating excessively, smoking, drinking too much alcohol, lack of exercise, overspending on material things (while not tithing or even contributing proportionally), filling your time with selfish activities while not attending to the needs of others, not exercising your responsibilities as a spouse, parent, or citizen, and so on. And this only scratches the surface of how God looks at things. We are expected to be perfect as our Father in heaven is perfect. Anything less is displeasing to Him.

God's anger is always an expression of His righteousness. All people on earth suffer the consequences of sin, all people age, all struggle, all get sick, all deteriorate, all die. But God uses the suffering of His people for positive purposes because He loves us. In Hebrews 12:7, the author writes, "It is for discipline that you have to endure. God is treating you as sons. For what son is there whom his father does not discipline?" We may be receiving some divine guidance from our hardship. Some discipline is direct cause-and-effect; that is, we did something displeasing and God is sending us a message. The cause may be a single event or an unacceptable lifestyle. But more often, our hardship has a deeper purpose for the good of our faith or His kingdom.

For Christians, sorrow and difficulty comes with a silver lining, with compassion, and with restraint. While on earth, we know our difficulty has meaning. God uses that difficulty to shape us and those we love. If we examine our hardships objectively, we will find God doing His work in us and through us for others. Oftentimes, our hardships draw us closer to our Lord or strengthen those close to us. Maybe the hardship is not for us or our family at all; it may be to create a circumstance for you to shine your light—your faith—to others as a witness during difficult times. God uses hardship for His purpose. Sometimes we can find that good or purpose, many times we cannot. That is when we need to trust God when He says in Romans 8:28 that "we know that for those who love God all things work together for good."

There is another promise that resonates in 1 Corinthians 10:13: "No temptation has overtaken you that is not common to man. God is faithful, and He will not let you be tempted beyond your ability, but with the temptation He will also provide the way of escape, that you may be able to endure it." God knows us; the very hairs on our head are numbered (Matthew 10:30). He knows what we are capable of enduring and resisting by His grace. He will not send us more trouble or temptation than He does anyone else in the world and will not send us more than we can handle. Then it is up to us to resist and to call on the Spirit for help and faith.

God's anger with us, and our sin, is totally justified because of His perfection. While we deserve hardship and death, believers live in the assurance of God's love and grace in Christ. We know our hardships have a purpose and will result in a stronger relationship with our God all our lives. While that is hard to remember at the time, remember the words of 2 Timothy 2:11–13: "The saying is trustworthy, for: If we have died with Him, we will also live with Him; if we endure, we will also reign with Him; if we deny Him, He also will deny us; if we are faithless, He remains faithful—for He cannot deny Himself."

For Christians, sorrow and difficulty comes with a silver lining, with compassion, and with restraint. While on earth, we know our difficulty has meaning. God uses that difficulty to shape us and those we love.

Prayer: Dear God, I deserve Your anger over my sins, and I'm sorry. Thank You for sending Your Son, Jesus, to live and die for me. Send Your Holy Spirit, so that what I do and say may be pleasing in Your sight. I ask this through Christ, my Lord. Amen.

Wednesday

1. How do you respond when someone points out a mistake, or worse, a sin in your life?

2. If God is aware even of your secret sins, from whom are you hiding them?

3. Who stands to benefit most by an exposé of your "secret sins"?

4. It is often said that no one knows how long he has to live. Do you think Moses would agree?

5. Given the brevity of life (v. 10), how should you approach the hours of the coming day?

Psalm 90:11-12

Who considers the power of Your anger, and Your wrath according to the fear of You? So teach us to number our days that we may get a heart of wisdom.

A Heart of Wisdom

When I was in my late teens and early twenties, I recall having anger management issues. I guess I wasn't any different than any other guy my age, then or now, but it always got me in trouble. When the dog ate my retainer (because I left it on the coffee table, stupid dog), I hit a closet door in my dad's house, leaving a rather large hole. I caught heck for that one and had to restore the door to its original condition. A few years later when I was married with children, I was frustrated at one of my toddler-aged kids and closed the sliding glass door so hard it shattered into a million pieces (I counted), which I had to clean up and pay to replace; payback for being immature, I'm sure. I even remember a time when my wife and I moved from one house to another. I removed a hook-rug from the wall on moving day just to find a fist hole behind it. I wondered to myself, when did that happen? Great! Now I have to run to the hardware store to buy spackle and paint for a house we had already sold!

I sure am glad that our almighty God controls His temper. Can you imagine the lightning bolts flying and fist holes we would see if He let loose every time we messed up? A person could understandably interpret Psalm 90 as describing a God that is hurtful and vengeful. The words are very strong: "return man to dust" (v. 3), "sweep them away as with a flood" (v. 5), "brought to an end by Your anger" and "by Your wrath we are dismayed" (v. 7), and "bring our years to an end like a sigh" (v. 9). Such is the finality of sinful man's life in the hands of a God who is just and righteous. Yet, as much as we have it coming to us, Christians live lives of hope and blessing. Yes, our sins deserve God's full wrath. But God's love in the person of Jesus steps in and takes those heavy blows for us in His Passion and on His cross. God's blessings through Christ might not be recognizable by the world's standards, but they are most certainly there for those who trust in Christ by faith. Even if our years on earth are difficult, we know during those years we are saved. We do not need to

163

do anything to attain salvation. Our God has provided it without any merit or worthiness on our part. We should therefore live godly lives in response to our eternal salvation won for us by our Savior.

God's wrath takes the form of hardship, disease, and—ultimately—death. Yet it is not inflicted on targeted people as a knee-jerk reaction, like punching a wall or slamming a door. It is an ongoing condition of life after sin. While God hates sin, He does not cause evil or even foster it. And for those of us who believe, God allows hardship to occur for our good—"discipline," Paul calls it—but not as punishment for sin. Today's verses state that His wrath is as great as the fear He is owed. The word "fear" in this context has a different connotation than its modern meaning. Today, we equate fear with anxiety and being afraid or terrified about something. In the Bible, "fear" means having a sense of reverence and trust in God that includes total commitment to Him. In proportional response, we should therefore have as much reverence, trust, and commitment to God as He has anger about our sin. In fact, we do, because God has given us the gift of faith, which trusts in Christ for salvation, and His perfect love, which casts out our being afraid. We can rest confidently in Christ, knowing that our salvation is complete and our eternal destiny secured.

Sometimes I wonder why we are left in this world to toil for so long when going home to heaven would be far better. The Apostle Paul answers this Philippians 1:22–24, "If I am to live in the flesh, that means fruitful labor for me. Yet which I shall choose I cannot tell. I am hard pressed between the two. My desire is to depart and be with Christ, for that is far better. But to remain in the flesh is more necessary on your account." Paul knew he had work to do for God on this earth, and the statement holds true for us as well.

Anger is not the only topic covered in the verses assigned for today. Moses also prays for God to teach us how to number our days rightly, so that we might have wise hearts. That almost serves as a prelude to the conclusion of our psalm, which we'll look at tomorrow. Psalm 90 presents the contrast between the eternity of God and the temporary nature of our earthly, human existence. Now, I'm not denying the existence of our immortal soul, it's just that Moses is hitting us between the eyes with the fact that our time in earth is short. Have you ever heard of "taking the long view" of something? Moses is encouraging us to walk wisely in the proper fear of God (fear, love, and trust in God, Martin Luther would say), so that, knowing that our days are limited, we keep our eternal life with God always in view. Through His Word of both Law and Gospel, God will teach us and give us a wise heart.

Men, it is one thing to be a passive participant at church and to be a non-participating "believer" the rest of the week. It's quite another thing to be engaged in worship and prayer, witness and service, not only on Sunday but also throughout the week. By His grace, God enables us to exercise our faith. God enables us to live our faith, study His Word, and bring others to the knowledge of Jesus by our love, our actions, and our witness. Today's petition for the Holy Spirit to help us number our days aright and gain a heart of wisdom, a wisdom that comes only from God's Word, means both knowledge and practice. In other words, God enables us to make an eternal difference in this world.

....

Men, it is one thing to be a passive participant at church. . . It's quite another thing to be engaged in worship and prayer, witness and service, not only on Sunday but also throughout the week.

Prayer: Heavenly Father, I have not always valued the significance of each day that You have given me. Help me to order my days rightly, so that making use of Your grace and blessing in Your Word, I may have a wise heart. In Jesus' name I pray. Amen.

....

Thursday

Daily Study Questions
Psalm 90:11–12

1. When is it all right to be angry?

2. Are you ever afraid of God? What role do you think fear of God should play in the life of a Christian?

3. What relationship might there be between people thinking that God is unfair and people's inability to recognize the depth of their sin?

4. What does it mean to number your days? How would doing this lead to greater wisdom?

5. If you are saved by grace through faith in Christ alone, why should you try to present "a heart of wisdom" to God?

Psalm 90:13–17

Return, O Lord! How long? Have pity on Your servants! Satisfy us in the morning with Your steadfast love, that we may rejoice and be glad all our days. Make us glad for as many days as You have afflicted us, and for as many years as we have seen evil. Let Your work be shown to your servants, and Your glorious power to their children. Let the favor of the Lord our God be upon us, and establish the work of our hands upon us; yes, establish the work of our hands!

The Work of Our Hands

Let's play Password. Here are your hints: the day I was married, when I got my first car, the births of my children, obtaining a career goal, my daughter's wedding, obtaining my MBA, and my kids' graduations. So, what's your guess? If you said "things that bring joy," you would be right. Here are some other hints: diagnosed with stage-one cancer, in a car accident, lost a parent, laid off from work, short of money to make monthly payments. If I had given these hints instead of the former, would you still have guessed "things that bring joy"? For Christians, that should be true. Thank God, it was not advanced cancer; praise the Lord, the accident was not worse; hallelujah, my parent is with Jesus; praise God, I finally received the shove I needed to get out of my job rut; thank the Lord, without cable, we spend more time as a family.

How do you react to hardship?

Joy is not something that someone can give you. It comes from within. It may be in response to external conditions, but it still comes from down inside you. It is a gift of the Holy Spirit that resides in your heart. Even hardships can be sources of joy to God's people because it is through the circumstances of our lives that we are drawn to our Lord and His service. The whole Psalm 90 prayer is an acknowledgement of God's righteousness, our resulting sinful condition, and our dependency on His grace and mercy to make life on earth tolerable, constructive, and fulfilling.

During our study this week, we have reflected on God's righteous anger and

167

the resulting condition of our sinful lives. This is not the most positive and uplifting chapter in the Bible. In fact, it can be downright scary and depressing. But here's the thing: God loves us and shows His compassion for us every day. Yes, we have issues, conflict, pain, and sorrow; but we also have joy, happiness, and above all, hope. We have the hope of eternal life through faith in Jesus. We have the knowledge that no matter what happens to us, God will get us through it and never give us more than we can handle.

Moses wraps up his prayer asking God to make us glad for what He has given us. A popular song lyric recently stated we should not "always have what we want, but want what we have." In other words, be satisfied and joyful. As the poster says, "If we are walking on thin ice, we might as well dance." We should live each day to the fullest and find the good in everything. God blesses us through sorrow and bounty.

Stop and think of a time in your life when something started out to be a terrible occurrence and ended up being the best thing that ever happened. In 2006, my job as vice president was eliminated for organizational reasons. I loved my job! Forget the fact that I had founded my division twelve years before; forget that I had been totally committed to its success; and forget that I compromised other areas of my life to support my division. Even though the company was gracious enough to offer me a comparable position in another area, it was not a job doing what I wanted to do, so I opted out.

It was then that I was led (inspired? positioned? pushed?) by God to start a company. Three years later, our income has improved, we have more flexibility to serve and volunteer (or write Bible studies), and my wife and I have never been closer. God has also grown our dependence on Him to support us with business and customers. It was very scary at first not knowing where the next project and related income would come from. But we knew that God had always provided, and we did not expect anything to change as long as we trusted and put it in His hands. Deuteronomy 8:18 states in part, "You shall remember the LORD your God, for it is He who gives you power to get wealth." Worst case, things do not work out and God opens another employment opportunity—so far so good.

The last verse of our psalm has a great message. "Establish the work of our hands upon us." Most men (and women) wear many hats. We have many roles and responsibilities concurrently and consecutively. We are fathers, sons, brothers, husbands, employers, employees, friends, neighbors, mentors, sponsors, coaches, and so on. In all we do, others should see God in us. We should fulfill each responsibility to the best of our ability and perform it with a right heart. 1 Timothy 5:8 states, "If anyone does not provide for his relatives, and especially for members of his household, he has denied the faith and is worse than an unbeliever." Nevertheless, it is our gracious Lord who establishes the work of our hands. There is nothing He calls us to do in which He does not also give us the tools we need to do it.

With God's grace, we can also be content with what God has led us to do. That is not to say we should not strive to improve, but not everyone is blessed to be wealthy, an artist, a leader, a craftsman, and so on. Nevertheless, we all have God-given skills and talents that should be applied to the established "work of our hands." Paul goes on to say in 1 Timothy 6:6–8, "Now there is great gain in godliness with contentment, for we brought nothing into the world, and we cannot take anything out of the world. But if we have food and clothing, with these we will be content." God will indeed provide for our every need.

So often, we launch an initiative and ask God to bless it. Sometimes it happens for us. Other times, His answer is no and the effort is not blessed. We may never know why, but things go south. This even occurs in church work; for example, a ministry fails for some reason. We try to do something good but it does not seem to go anywhere.

This is where prayer is critical, knowing that God hears and answers our prayers for the sake of Jesus. We can request discernment, guidance, and wisdom. We need to be quiet long enough to hear and feel what God is saying and where He is leading. Our prayer should not be "Lord, please bless what we are trying to do"; rather, it should be "Lord, please lead us to do what You are blessing." God's got the master plan, not us. We need Him to establish the work of our hands, and He will do it.

....

Not everyone is blessed to be wealthy, an artist, a leader, a craftsman, and so on. Nevertheless, we all have God-given skills and talents that should be applied to the established "work of our hands."

Prayer: Dear Holy Spirit, through Your Word, point out the ways that I have fallen short of God's will for my life. Renew my faith and strengthen me with all that I need to do. Bless the work of my hands so that I may be a blessing to others. In Jesus' name. Amen.

....

Friday

Daily Study Questions
Psalm 90:13–17

1. How is it possible that the man who wrote the desperate and hopeless previous verses of this psalm suddenly write a prayer that exudes confidence and hope?

2. How does verse 13 provide a powerful (and rhetorically impressive) counterpoint to verse 3?

3. In verse 9, the lament was the agony of living "all our days" under God's wrath; now verse 14 speaks about rejoicing "all our days." How can "all our days" contain both things—which is it?

4. Moses is content to ask for an equal payback of glad days to balance the days of sorrow and despair (v. 15). How does St. Paul push the radical hope of faith even further in Romans 8:18 and 2 Corinthians 4:17?

5. What assurance does verse 17 provide as you prepare for another day of doing what God gives you to do—your vocation?

Week Six

··

Psalm 90

··

The 90th psalm is a psalm of instruction in
which Moses teaches the origin of death, namely sin, which, though known only by God and
hidden from the world, is yet inborn in all from
Adam to us. It shows that life here is not only
short but also miserable, so that it may well be
called a daily death. Nevertheless, the psalmist
says that such a life is good, so that through
it we would be driven to see God's grace and
His help to deliver us from it all. For those who
never think of death and feel no misery remain
senseless fools, caring nothing for God's grace
or help. The psalm ends with the prayer that
God would show us His work, namely His deliverance from sin and death, that is, that He
would send Christ. And the psalmist asks that,
while we live here, God would establish our
work, that is, that both spiritual and worldly
authority may be and remain favorable. The
90th psalm is a short, fine, rich, and full little
prayer.

-Martin Luther

Week Six, Psalm 90
GROUP BIBLE STUDY
(Questions and answers are on pp. 219–22.)

1. Under what circumstances do you feel especially small and insignificant next to the grandeur and immensity of the universe?

2. What does the opening of the psalm (v. 2) teach us about the relationship between God and His creation?

3. Think about the wider culture and then about the Church's culture; what evidence of man's effort to deny death's reality do you see in each? Why does Moses, with such zeal, drive home the point of man's mortality and futility?

4. Which of the metaphors for man's impermanence and insignificance (vv. 3–6) seems the most powerful or effective? What metaphors might a twenty-first-century psalmist use to convey the same message?

5. The appalling tragedy of verse 6 is that what starts with such promise and even beauty so quickly disintegrates into death, decay, and nothingness. Is this pathetic perspective on life appropriate in a Christian worldview, or is this merely morbid and unworthy of the optimism that should define the lives of God's people?

OKAY TO COPY THIS PAGE.

6. There is a reason for the emptiness and despair that are at the heart of every human life. How do verses 7 and 8 fit with the preceding verses? Why is it that the wrath of God seems to be so seldom mentioned (much less seriously considered), even in Christian churches?

7. Why is it that men like to fancy themselves in the role of a cowboy or swashbuckler who goes out with his boots on in a blaze of glory? How does the psalmist portray the end of life in verse nine? Which account is more accurate? Why do you think men are so inclined to recast the grim realities that attend death?

8. Overall, the psalmist presents a pointed and painfully frank assessment of the place and significance of man in the universe. While we may be forced grudgingly to admit the truth of what he presents, we may have doubts about what to do with the information. Should these hard truths be a prominent component of the church's message? Should it be a regular theme in preaching, or is this one of those doctrines that is better left in the textbooks and not openly discussed?

9. What is God's work that is mentioned in verse 16, and what does that work have to do with the work that we do (v. 17)?

10. In the not-so-distant past, this psalm was considered a standard text to be read at the funerals of Christian people. Do you think the psalm is appropriate to such an occasion? Why do you think that the psalm is no longer used with such regularity? Would it be a good text for a confirmation sermon, or at a wedding?

Small-Group Leader Guide

This guide will help guide you in discovering the truths of God's Word. It is not, however, exhaustive, nor is it designed to be read aloud during your session.

1. Before you begin, spend some time in prayer, asking God to strengthen your faith through a study of His Word. The Scriptures were written so that we might believe in Jesus Christ and have life in His name (John 20:31). Also, pray for participants by name.

2. Before your meeting, review the session material, read the Bible passages, and answer the questions in the spaces provided. Your familiarity with the session will give you confidence as you lead the group.

3. As a courtesy to participants, begin and end each session on time.

4. Have a Bible dictionary or similar resource handy to look up difficult or unfamiliar names, words, and places. Ask participants to help you in this task. Be sure that each participant has a Bible and a study guide.

5. Ask for volunteers to read introductory paragraphs and Bible passages. A simple "thank you" will encourage them to volunteer again.

6. See your role as a conversation facilitator rather than a lecturer. Don't be afraid to give participants time to answer questions. By name, thank each participant who answers; then invite other input. For example, you may say, "Thank you, Al. Would anyone else like to share?"

7. Now and then, summarize aloud what the group has learned by studying God's Word.

8. Remember that the questions provided are discussion starters. Allow participants to ask questions that relate to the session. However, keep discussions on track with the session.

9. Everyone is a learner! If you don't know the answer to a question, simply tell participants that you need time to look at more Scripture passages or to ask your pastor.

Monday Psalm 44:1–3

1. While it is not necessarily a sign of great spirituality, some people will attest to frequent experiences of hearing God speak. These experiences must be approached with care, as God is not the only one "speaking" to us. God's voice is discerned by its conformity to the explicit revelation He gives in holy Scripture.

2. Looking back from the period of the Davidic monarchy, the time of Moses and Joshua (exodus and conquest) probably seemed almost like ancient history. (It would have been at least 500 years in the past!) But those were the glory days of Israel's history when God acted to save.

3. The exodus marks *the* gospel moment in the whole of the Old Testament. This event is God intervening for His people—rescuing them from a dreadful reality and giving them what they could never expect or earn—a land, a name, a future hope. The results of the exodus were still daily experienced by every Israelite living in the Promised Land as one of God's chosen people.

4. We are able to keep our own expectations and spiritual standards in check when we recall that God typically works in ordinary and mundane ways. The vast majority of God's people have always lived *between* the dramatic and spectacular displays of God's intervening power. Like us, they learned to be content with the memory and the promise of God's salvific action on their behalf.

5. Not only do we relate the great stories of our faith—Israel, Jesus, and the restoration of the resurrection—but we also include the stories of our own lived experiences of God's faithful grace at work in our lives . . . both the spectacular and rare and the mundane and regular.

Tuesday Psalm 44:4–8

1. God's action of winning a victory for you may have been spectacular or quite ordinary—such divine interventions don't always look like "miracles"; but faith recognizes the reality of God's action behind the win, whether academic, athletic, relational, or spiritual.

2. The relationship between Israel's kings and God as their King had a rocky beginning (you can read about it in 1 Samuel 8–12). A divine monarchy didn't need a human king, yet God agreed to the people's demand for a king and gave them Saul and then David and his lineage. The psalmist actually had two kings—a human one, and God,

who was the real authority even behind the earthly monarch.

3. If God does the fighting, then shouldn't we just stay out of His way and do nothing? This age-old question gets to the fundamental root of the interface between God's work for us and our responsibility to live as faithful creatures who use their gifts and skills to accomplish God's purposes. The psalmist is not implying an either/or choice but is giving ultimate credit where it is due.

4. While most Christians enjoy living under the illusion of universal love and would like to think that they are friends with all and enemies of none (doesn't Jesus tell us to live this way?), Scripture makes it clear that when God is your Lord, you will have enemies. People who are threatened by a creating and judging God are threatened by God's people. (Check out 1 John 2–3 for more on the animosity between Christ's people and the world's citizens.)

5. A challenge on almost any front can be better met and more confidently addressed by relying on God's faithful provision of the longed-for victory. Such a perspective also cultivates the virtues of humility and God-dependence that are hallmarks of Christian faith.

Wednesday Psalm 44:9–16

1. Whatever the circumstances, the greatest sting is usually attached to the barb that attacks our own sense of worth and value, causing us to despair of our own abilities and even doubt our identity.

2. The psalmist quite rightly gives credit where credit is due and recognizes that God is finally the one planning and orchestrating every circumstance—even the difficult ones.

3. It seems that the best way to understand the psalm is at face value—the same people on the same day are being described. The God who works victories also brings humiliation, and sometimes at the same time. Most Christians encounter this tension on a regular (daily!?) basis. We rarely encounter altogether pure circumstances but receive life as a mixture of joy and sorrow, honor and shame.

4. While not everyone experiences outright attacks from those opposed to Christ and His truth, all Christians living in the West are aware of the sometimes subtle but always relentless dismissal of spiritual truth by those who are powerful and respected in the world. That God would tolerate such disregard for this truth is a mystery, indeed, but is reflective of His long-suffering and patient character as He yearns to call all—even the prideful and arrogant—to Himself.

5. Empty and in despair: this is where the Law always leaves us. But this is precisely the place that the Christian desperately needs to be because, from this position of utter helplessness and failure, God is eager to intervene with the Word of grace in Christ. The Gospel is always God's last word and the only contender able to overcome the Law.

Thursday Psalm 44:17–22

1. Dark times may relate to work or finances, or they may be related to great health challenges. Of course, some of the darkest, but least recognized, seasons may have more to do with family relationships and struggles that seem routine.

2. Trying times emotionally and spiritually can work in opposite ways in our lives. The same event(s) can push us closer to God—there is nowhere else to turn—or drive us away from God—we look, but can't seem to see His guiding hand. Of course, sometimes the same event will have both results almost simultaneously.

3. The psalmist asserts that he and his fellow Israelites have not been faithless: they have kept the covenant and upheld what God had called them to do. Thus, it appears to him that God is being horribly unjust and is failing to do what He had promised. If they had been unfaithful, he avers, then he could better understand the difficulties they were experiencing (vv. 20–21)

4. The fact that God knows everything means that He thoroughly knows all that we are experiencing—even the hardships—and further knows the sincerity of our motives and faith. Yet He allows us to endure what seems to be unfair and intolerable difficulties. We might be led to conclude that if God knows everything, then He should know better than to allow what is happening!

5. A reality check is always beneficial to Christians who are too often lulled into believing lies about a life of ease and comfort. That we will experience challenges and pain and sorrow—and these even straight from the loving hand of God—arms us for the battle that each day brings. We are not caught unaware or unprepared. We are steeled to the inevitable onslaught of life, and we are ready to cling to God and His promises, even when His hand is delivering the onslaught. To be driven more fully into God's grasp is always a good thing.

Friday Psalm 44:23–26

1. While it is true that as we mature we tend not to long with the same yearning for "the next thing," the fact is that there is always another stage yet to come—sometimes, though, it may not be as good or as pleasant as the present.

2. This gets at the difference between contentment and complacency. While we

should be content with our current lot, we should never become complacent and forget that God has promised more—the final fulfillment of all things at Christ's second coming. At the same time, we can't allow our wish for what's next to lead us to miss the joy and needs of the present.

3. Clearly, the psalmist is confident enough of his relationship with Yahweh that he feels free to call his God to task, fully expecting God to do what He has promised to do. While it is certainly possible for such praying to take on the character of impatient whining and even impertinent irreverence, in the context of the psalm—the context of complete faith and trust—the words actually reflect faith in the God who will do what He has promised. The psalmist is appealing to God's mercy to bring such action sooner and not later.

4. Made from dust, man returns to dust. To use the terms of dust and ground (earth) is to remind us of our mortality and to point out the gravity of the calamity that was oppressing the writer. Effectively, he is asserting that death is the next stop in this unnamed tragedy of sorrow.

5. The final word is steadfast love. It is here, at last, that psalmist rests, and it is here that we must rest even in the face of life's most distressing and trying challenges. God's mercy, His *chesed*, His steadfast love does not waver or diminish. This is the frame and foundation for all of life—even the agony of life.

1. *When do you feel the most secure and safe? What factors contribute significantly to this feeling? What things pose the greatest threat to that sense of well-being and security?*

Perhaps it is being at home with a content family gathered around; or maybe it is positive affirmation from your boss, or a robust earnings report on your retirement plan. Whether it is financial or familial or spiritual, we need to recognize that there are things we count on and look to for a sense of security and well-being in our lives.

2. *How is the conquest of Canaan (described in v. 2) a cause of hope and a source of comfort for the psalmist? How can remembering past blessings from God provide you with present comfort and security? What events from your past give you present hope?*

God's work of settling His chosen people in the Promised Land was a continual source of encouragement for those people in every generation that followed—it was the proof of God's faithfulness and love for them. Similarly, the salvific events of God on your own behalf can serve to remind you of God's continued presence and promise.

3. *How important is the Church's work of telling the story of God's love and actions for His people? How should the Church do this work?*

Telling the story faithfully is what Paul was talking about when he told Christians to cling to what he had given to them and to pass it along to others (1 Corinthians 11:2; 15:1–5). This task is far more significant than people realize, and it is done well simply in the reading of Scripture in the Divine Service, in the Sunday School classroom, and on the edge of a child's bed as a Bible story is read at bedtime. Rehearsing God's faithfulness means sharing the tradition that has been given and recognizing that in God's story, our stories finally have meaning.

4. *People use many images to convey their understanding of God: grandfather, friend, counselor, hero, etc. How does the image of God as king (v. 4) change one's view of God? How might this image impact a person's view of his relationship with God?*

Recognizing God's authority as King will check a sense of over-familiarity that is not appropriately respectful of God as Creator and Lord. No one image of God adequately captures all that needs to be said about God and our relationship with Him.

5. What does it mean to spend a day boasting in God? How can we justify such boasting when God calls us to be humble and to reject all arrogance?

First, boasting in God is not arrogant—it is holy worship! To speak of God's majesty and glory is always fitting for God's creatures. Second, this boasting can be verbal, but it is also expressed in a life lived confidently according to the promises of God. To boast in God is to give Him due credit for every blessing and to take Him at His word—trusting His forgiveness and His provision.

6. What does the image of a sheep cheaply sold for butchering (vv. 11–12) convey about the worth of a human being? Is there any sense in which this graphic and disquieting image is still applicable for Christians?

The thought of God entering the market ready to unload a worthless sheep to the first buyer to make a offer is not particularly encouraging—especially when the sheep is emblematic of God's chosen people. Indeed, the picture is terrifying. Yet the picture is true. Even those in Christ have no value in themselves, and are, by rights, destined for the same ignominious auction block of judgment.

7. Can God's people expect any special treatment when it comes to the hassles and hurts that define life in this world? How is it possible that being one of God's people may actually invite more *pain and sorrow?*

The psalmist exemplifies the reality that even God's people struggle through some mighty difficulties. Bearing the name of Christ does not provide one with a free pass from sorrow or pain; it actually guarantees that there will be trouble, as God only disciplines those He counts as sons (Hebrews 12:6). Sometimes it is *because* we are God's sons that we experience God's hard judgment.

8. What do you say to fellow Christians who do not understand how God can be so slow to answer their prayers or apparently unwilling to spare them from sorrow and pain in spite of their faithfulness?

The psalm reminds us of the hard truth that there is no special pleading or free passes even for God's people. The psalm effectively discredits all efforts to proclaim a gospel of prosperity ("God wants you to be rich and healthy and happy . . . just ask and believe" or some similar nonsense). Even doing right is no guarantee of blessing. So, one finds comfort as St. Paul did (who quotes our psalm in Romans 8:36): even when we are feeling like sheep led to the slaughter, God is in control and continues to work all things according to His plan, which is our final and ultimate good.

9. Why do you think Psalm 44 (and others like it) with its dark tone and sometimes-pessimistic attitude is included in the Psalter? What benefit is there in studying this psalm?

Besides the simple fact that they are brutally honest and accurately reflect the reality of life, the Psalms also compel us to remember that we are not in control of life and that even when life is unraveling and rising up against us, God *is* still in control. No circumstance of life, no matter how tragic or evil, can alter that fact.

10. What attitude or life changes does the message of this psalm demand of you? How will it affect the way that you face the week's challenges or the way that you work to encourage others?

Perhaps the psalm forces you to rethink some of your assumptions about how the Christian life is "supposed" to look. You need to allow a little more room for what is sad or difficult or unpleasant. Perhaps the psalm will help you to be more sensitive to the genuine hurts of others and the resultant struggles they face as they attempt to reconcile their faith with their reality. Ultimately, of course, the psalm should drive you firmly into the steadfast love of God—the only hope when life turns sour.

Week Two, Psalm 74
Daily Study Questions

Monday Psalm 74:1–3

1. The author of the devotion is right: the very word *politics* has a decidedly pejorative connotation in the lexicon of American English. Yet politics is simply the word that describes our working together in community to accomplish things. A father makes political decisions when he takes into account the impact of a decision on each member of his family. A husband can make a politically savvy decision when he considers how his wife's family will interpret his actions. Both of these amount to truly political decisions.

2. This is something most of us typically take for granted. We don't think much about *how* we decide things or why we prioritize some things over others. Honest and ongoing reflection on your decision matrix may reveal some surprising motivations that you had not previously recognized and may lead to some re-prioritizing.

3. Because of his faith in God, the psalmist is perplexed about what God is not doing. It makes no sense that the God who loves His people Israel would allow that people to be so utterly devastated by such an ungodly enemy. Essentially, the writer of the psalm wants to know what factors are at work in God's decision to allow the ruin of Israel.

4. Although the psalmist is asking deeply probing and deeply troubling questions, at least he is asking! And while is giving specific counsel on the course he believes God should take, he is yet in conversation with God. At the most distressing moment—the complete destruction of the nation—the psalmist does not reject his faith but clings all the more to the only hope he has left.

5. With the psalmist, when the crisis is severe, the Christian needs to learn to turn to God and not away from God. Vibrant and dynamic faith is most necessary when confronting life's hard realities. Consideration of God's centrality in one's own life story must be the core of a believer's way of deciding anything.

Tuesday Psalm 74:4–7

1. This world seems to do a capable job of humbling its residents. Whether it is a vista across the land or into the depths of space, or the awareness of the complexity of life and the puniness of man, the lessons of man's mortality, life's brevity, and ambition's futility; all conspire to make us realize that our final position is as desperate as Israel's at the fall of Jerusalem.

2. The psalm gives a graphic description of the razing of Solomon's great temple. The ensigns or signs of Babylonian military might have replaced the signs of God's blessing and grace (Aaron's budding rod and golden censers, Numbers 16:38; 17:10). The gold plating is smashed—perhaps to facilitate its recovery and plundering before the remaining shattered wood is put to the torch. And all of this is done to the sound of bellowing Babylonians, whose victory cry is Israel's lament. The details of the account have all the markings of an eyewitness report.

3. If God can do this to His own chosen city and to His own dwelling, then no one can foolishly claim a place of privilege or exemption from His judgment and wrath. We are all vulnerable—liable to fall, likely to wander from God's plan. Israel rejected God's plan and paid dearly for their folly and sin. So will all who step off the path of God's will for His creatures.

4. While it may not always feel like you are encompassed by sworn enemies bent on your destruction, the basic reality of the world in rebellion against God and God's people will not change. Those who are not God's people cannot help it—they hate God and all who follow God.

5. Of course, this question is not easily answered and has generated debate in the Church right to the present. The psalmist offers a fine example, however. Sometimes (actually all the time . . . ?) there is nothing you can do but cry to God and beg for His mercy. Defense of His Church and His people is, after all, God's job, one that He will do in His time and in His way. Still, it is clear that such threats should not provoke fear in God's people; the better reaction is sorrow and repentance—not fear, and not anger or revenge.

Wednesday Psalm 74:8–11

1. While our God-given instincts to defend the helpless and to cheer for the underdog may prompt us to act on their behalf, the inherent risk is that these people are in no position to reward or reciprocate. In other words, even if the "rescue" is successful, there is no tangible, material result. In the world's terms, helping the helpless is nonsense.

2. Nothing. And to state the obvious, this is precisely the baffling wonder of God's grace—it is absurd and beautiful.

3. In one sense, they have nothing to do with each other. God does not need time to see if His people are worth saving or to consider whether the benefit of intervention on their behalf is worth the cost to Himself. God does not bide His time while He waits for His people to work themselves to a level where they are worthy

of His grace. He risks, He loves, He intervenes simply because that is His nature. It has nothing to do with us. On the other hand, God does not intervene on behalf of the self-reliant and proud. Grace and divine aid are *only* for the downtrodden and impotent. The long waiting period before His intervention does have something to do with the people—it is intended to bring the people to full repentance.

4. The psalmist complains that God is not taking action and, worse, without a prophet, He is not even responding to the prayers imploring His action. The psalmist does not understand, but he continues to pray anyway. When God is silent—and silent much too long—there is only one right response: continue to pray to the only source of hope.

5. Perhaps there is literally nothing you can do but pray, and so you simply continue to do that. In the meantime, however, you recognize that it is *not* necessarily a sign of God's disfavor that the problem continues unchecked. Remember Israel's distress and the years that dragged by with no indication of God's presence, much less His intervention. God's people do suffer in difficult situations, and they do still receive His grace, even in those situations. Our attitude should be one that is willing to endure what God deems necessary—even if quite unpleasant.

Thursday Psalm 74:12–17

1. Perhaps you are tempted to remain silent, and even give tacit agreement to a false idea, when you are at work and seek the approval or camaraderie of the group. Or maybe it is when you are with family members and don't want to cause any tension.

2. Christians accept the veracity and authority of the Bible because they know and trust their Lord. In other words, the foundation of our faith is Christ, not the Bible. We rely on Scripture because it testifies to Christ and because our Lord taught us by word and example to count on the word of Scripture. Thus, Christians don't have to be in the business of proving the veracity of the Bible. When pressed on their view of the Bible, the best response is not defense of the text but proclamation of Christ and His reality. To trust Christ is to trust His Word—spoken and written. It is just that simple.

3. Like the Christian, the writer of the psalm knows what God has done for him and for His people (vv. 12–17). It is God's actions in history that provide the assurance of God's ongoing and future provision for His people. The events of creation and exodus demonstrated God's sovereignty over all that exists—such a God can easily contend with an invading army and a despondent people.

4. Even aspects of life that were troublesome, frightening, and threatening—like

night and winter (all the more terrifying in the ancient world with its lack of technological defenses against darkness and cold)—had to submit to God's rule.

5. Verse 12 makes clear that the actions of God have a goal: they work deliverance; they are for the good of God's people. The same "King . . . from of old" is still at work in the present century, and with the same purpose. He works for your deliverance, and He can surely handle any of the monsters that threaten you—even those that dwell within.

Friday Psalm 74:18-23

1. You may or may not believe that you live in a world that is dominated by the corruption of sin and its violence. However, it is undoubtedly true that the person who would deny this reality has no concept of what this world is supposed to look like when every corner of it has not been permeated with the perversion of sin! It takes little reflection to realize that such dark places abound (a few minutes of the nightly news will remove all illusions of peace and tranquility).

2. The psalmist is concerned first, with God's name (v. 18). His primary desire is to see God honored and His name revered. It is always the mark of faith that it is less concerned with its own welfare than it is with God's glory and praise.

3. The covenant was God's idea. By it, He had bound Himself to His people, and although the people had persistently and perennially failed to uphold any of their part of the covenant, the psalmist calls on God to fulfill His covenant word and save His people. Christians have the benefit of even greater promises, delivered by Word and Sacrament, by which God binds Himself to His people and pledges His grace and action on their behalf.

4. When we try to "explain" why God has done or not done something, we invariably end up in trouble—sometimes we end up in outright heresy. Hence, it is wisest to allow God to make His own case—that is, don't offer explanations but instead review the history of God's actions for His people, and reiterate the promises He has made and allow these realities to provide a sufficient account of what God may be doing presently. God pleads His own cause when He acts and provides incontrovertible proof of His love and grace. This result always comes to pass . . . in God's time. Those who are still waiting for the plan to unfold are wise to wait without making attempts to vindicate God's plan and timing.

5. The psalm provides a stirring example of heartfelt entreaty coupled with profound praise and teaches the value of "historical remembering" as a way of praising God and seeking His help. Further, the psalm helps us with our focus as we are led to pray especially for the downtrodden and afflicted. Praying with passion for God's honor, for

God's truth, for God's Church, and for final justice would likely be appropriate new additions in the prayer lives of many Christians.

1. What is the worst destruction you have personally experienced or witnessed?

The question is vague by intention and could allow responses that range from natural disasters to traffic accidents, from divorce to substance abuse, from economic ruin to war.

2. The psalmist specifically mentions Mount Zion and "the sanctuary" as scenes of damage and ruin. Why are these places so significant? What message would this have sent to the people?

Mount Zion was the location of the temple within Jerusalem's walls, and the sanctuary is but a name for this holy structure where God and man met. While the temple was a beautiful work of architectural achievement, a symbol of national identity, and a source of great pride, it was above all else the assurance of the covenant reality. The presence of the temple meant that God was still Israel's God and they were still His people. The destruction of the temple called all of that fundamental reality into question.

3. In the opening verses, the psalmist makes rather modest requests of God. For what does he hope and pray? Why might he be content to ask simply for this?

Essentially, the psalmist is only asking that God would remember and notice what was happening to His people. "Remember!" is the heart of the prayer—"Don't forget Your promise to us; don't forget what we are now enduring." Given the extent of the destruction and the implications it had for Israel's standing before God (does God even care anymore?), this prayer may well have seemed quite bold enough in the circumstances.

4. The psalm offers a striking and chilling picture of the temple's desecration and destruction—a frontal assault of Satan against the kingdom of God (vv. 4–7). What are some of the ways that Satan attacks God's Church in the twenty-first century? Are such frontal assaults a thing of the past?

God is chastening His people, but He is using Satan and Satan's pawns to accomplish His purpose. No doubt, there are occasions yet today when Satan makes bold attacks on the Church—one can think of the persecution that persists in the Muslim world as well as in places where Christian worship is discouraged or forbidden. And of course, there is the relentless battle against the Church and her truth that is waged by the culture at large. There is no shortage of examples of the world threatening, undermining, and attacking the Church and her message.

5. In verse 4, the psalmist mentions one desecration in particular: the fact that the Babylonian invaders had actually placed their banners of war and conquest, their military standards, in the sanctuary of the temple. What are some ways that the world's "standards" have been set up in God's sanctuary, and the roar of the heathen heard in God's courts?

More insidious than bold frontal attacks are the covert operations of Satan against Christ's Church—the standards of the enemy being brought into the Church in ways that are not noticed. It is crucial to remember that satanic attacks on the Church do not cease . . . never . . . ever. If the attack is not blatant or immediately apparent, special vigilance is required that one may rightly recognize the satanic game and operations before they accomplish their purpose. Your group will probably have several observations about ways in which the Church is attacked in subtle and apparently innocent ways—most of all, perhaps, by the way the world's way of thinking and being so easily finds its way into the Church's life. When the Church emulates the surrounding culture, it is far too common to hear a heathen accent in the Lord's courts and to recognize the world's standards hanging in the sanctuary.

6. The destruction of the temple was tragic, but it did not exhaust the problems besetting the psalmist. According to verse 9, what further difficulty compounded Israel's woes? Do Christians today experience this sort of problem?

The signs of God's presence—His promise to be with His people through the means of the temple and its worship practices—were obscured by the horrific intrusion of the invading army. Worse, there was no longer a prophet available who could speak God's truth and God's comfort to the people. They were left in isolation, without even a word of acknowledgment coming from the divine throne. Mercifully, Christians are not confronted with this sort of suffering. Through Scripture, through the pastoral office, through the Office of the Keys, God delivers His Word to His people. Because we have the further assurance of God's presence in the sacraments, we need never wonder about God's presence with us.

7. What is the name that is being reviled and spurned, seemingly forever, by the enemies of God? How does the confident declaration of Philippians 2:9–11 provide another perspective on this name and the duration of man's scorn of that name?

The name is the Tetragrammaton, YHWH, Jehovah, Yahweh, LORD: it is the name revealed to Moses at the burning bush and the name of God's covenant promise to His people. Paul declares that because of the Son's obedience that name, *the* divine name is applied to Jesus; this assures us that, in the end, there will be no one scoffing or mocking the name of the Lord. All will acknowledge His sovereignty; all will bow before His glory and majesty, some in love and praise, others in shock and terror.

8. How does the dramatic shift in subject and tone from verse 12 through verse 17 change the lament and prayers that precede and follow these verses? Why do these verses have such a focused interest on God's rule over water and its creatures?

The praise of God and His sovereign rule over creation contrasts starkly with the bitter lament of the previous verses, as well as the renewed pleading of the following verses. But the reminder of God's character and history of grace to His people casts the rest of the psalm in a different light. The petitions do not come from a heart of despair but from a position of faith. Honest admission of the depth of the dilemma does not alter the confidence of faith. Water was ever the symbol of evil in its chaotic and random destruction—a rebel against the order of the Creator, its inhabitants ferocious, mysterious, and uncontrollable. The Leviathan—the sea monster—was a favorite appellation for Egypt, which was despoiled and then crushed as the waters submitted and divided at the Red Sea only to obliterate the raging monster of Pharaoh's army. The waters of the deep and all its horrible monsters must yield to God's rule.

9. Which enemies, do you think, present the greatest threat to God's Church and its people? The psalmist, as usual, insists that such enemies are "foolish"—a word in Hebrew that means moral as well as intellectual deprivation. Is this still true in today's world? Why might many find it difficult to call such enemies "fools"?

The problem, of course, is that in our world—as in many previous times in the history of the world—it is the intellectual elite who are often the most outspoken critics of Christian faith and a worldview founded on God and God's Law as real and normative for all of human life. Nevertheless, God's judgment holds: the denial of God and His truth is the height of human arrogance—it is the ultimate folly. The Church today must ever bear this in mind as it contends with the relentless assaults from its well-educated, well-mannered, well-groomed, well-respected, well-connected enemies who are in the final analysis fools—and nothing else.

10. Why do you think the psalmist gives special attention to those who are "downtrodden . . . poor and needy"? Who are the downtrodden, poor, and needy today? How does the Church fulfill this concern?

God and His people have always been particularly concerned not with the high and mighty but with the lowly and powerless. This is a theme throughout both testaments of Scripture. The way that the Church treats its lowliest members is the clearest declaration of the character of the Church. Today, one must look beyond the statistics of poverty and not forget the unborn among the downtrodden and poor . . . nor those who are living in broken homes. The Church's "social concern" will encompass more than providing a meal to a sojourner of stocking the shelves of a food bank—excellent as these works may be. Of course, it is critical to realize that when the Christian is operating with the correct perspective, he will not fail to count himself among the poor and needy; such is the state of us all in the spiritual realm of our relationship with God. The plea for God to remember the downtrodden is a plea for God to remember us repentant and desperate sinners.

Monday Psalm 77:1–3

1. As the devotion notes, sometimes what starts as a simple circumstance is compounded by our own mistakes, foolishness, or inattention into a situation that is much worse.

2. Different situations no doubt promote different responses. Perhaps it is true that when the problems are mostly self-inflicted, it is more difficult to look to God for relief—we think that a problem we have created is a problem we can fix!

3. Asaph looks to God for help but gets silence in response; in fact, Asaph blames God for his loss of sleep and distress of soul. There are times when God doesn't respond as we expect Him to. Why this happens is best left as one of those questions without a good answer—a question, quite frankly, better left unasked.

4. If we are honest, we will admit that sometimes we actually enjoy feeling miserable! In fact, it may well be the case that there are times when we choose to continue in sorrow and despondency even when the comfort and hope we need are being offered in God's grace. To choose to be miserable is more than foolish—it is sinful.

5. It is wise to establish a plan—perhaps prayers during lunch, or listening to recordings of the Bible while driving, or printing a verse and carrying it in your pocket—that will remind you regularly through the day of the source of your hope during trials.

Tuesday Psalm 77:4–6

1. If you are like most men, the time spent actually contemplating God's past blessings in your life (before you get distracted by some other pressing or interesting train of thought!) is likely measured in single-digit minutes. Serious meditation is not a skill that most of us develop.

2. When we are busy working—even busy doing what we can to fix a mess—we can easily begin to trust and rely upon ourselves and fail to look to God for the help that is needed. It might be far better to be stunned into silence that quietly waits for God than to be busy working without God to make things right on your own.

3. Recalling the past serves as evidence of God's capacity to act and deliver blessings. Whether the remembering of your own history or the long history that stretches back into the same events the encouraged Asaph, reviewing God's track record should serve as an impetus to renewed hope and confidence.

4. The poetic interpretation of Asaph's song is intriguing and fruitful—likely this is not a specific melody or words he is remembering, but the "song of his life." In other words, his song is another way of speaking of his life story: the narrative of God's faithfulness, Asaph's failures, and God's unfailing love and provision—punctuated, of course, with all of the details that make Asaph's life song unique. Compose your lyrics, settle on a style, and then sing your song. (But please, for my sake, don't choose disco!)

5. Five minutes is a long time when it comes to listing blessings—but likely not nearly long enough. Taking the time to begin to concretely and specifically develop and rehearse your "faith story" with God, your "life song," is a vital tool to be used in keeping the right perspective in both difficult times and happy times. The litany of God's faithfulness played out in your memory can help to reorient your present attitude and actions.

Wednesday Psalm 77:7–9

1. Unfortunately, we all have too many stories of messes and even tragedies that resulted from a simple lapse of memory and nothing more. Forgetfulness is a human disposition that carries a hefty price tag.

2. It's disconcerting because while we know that the answer to these questions is supposed to be the resounding and emphatic "NO!" of faith, we realize that, in our own thoughts and experience, at least part of us wants to say, "Maybe . . . I don't know . . . I'm not sure anymore . . . " The questions forced on us by hard times can derail the steady progress of growing faith.

3. While God has certainly promised to be faithful and thus is guaranteed to keep every promise, the force of these questions is troubling because of us. The problem is not God but we ourselves. We can trust God, but we can't trust ourselves, and we know that by rights God should be delivering on none of these promises because we deserve none of them.

4. In truth, you don't turn them off! The questions will, inevitably, arise. The critical thing is what happens after the questions force their way into your thoughts. Do you answer them with God's truth and promises, or do you yield to the force of the circumstances and waver in your faith? Don't ignore or deny the questions. Answer them with God's truth.

5. Christians do face trials, and real questions about God's faithfulness and timing do demand answers. The only answer is the promise of God that triumphs over even the most logically compelling doubt or question about God's plan and goodness. The answer is the reality of what God has already accomplished for you—and that perfectly in Christ.

Thursday Psalm 77:10–15

1. Clearly, an arm and hammer is a mighty symbol of strength, but there are many choices: the Roman fasces, an eagle or a lion, an aircraft carrier, a royal scepter, a dollar sign. All of these convey different aspects of what we understand as power and strength.

2. These are the standard ancient symbols of strength and power—weapons were wielded with the right arm. So when Asaph remembers God's right hand, he is remembering the strength and saving power of God, who works for the sake of His people.

3. It is as simple as beginning at Genesis and working forward. From the splendor and wonder of creation, to the rescue of Noah, the call of Abraham, the provision through Joseph, and finally to the climax of the exodus, it is clear that God has done tremendous things for the sake of His people.

4. God always intervenes for His people to give them what they need—whether release from Egyptian oppressors or release from the futility and hopelessness of sin. At Calvary, God acted quite consistently—giving Himself fully for the sake of His creation—acting mightily for the good of His people. The surprise is to learn to see the cross not as God's impotence but as the raw display of God's most potent and formidable force—His love.

5. The important thing for our Christian lives is learning to integrate our faith's realities into our daily routines. That God has triumphed with His mighty arm and won victory and salvation for His people is the consistent message of God's Word. That same power is now at work in your daily reality. Remembering this can alter how you think about every person and every challenge that you encounter.

Friday Psalm 77:16–20

1. While there seem to be descriptions of a rather severe thunderstorm, complete with some degree of cyclone or whirlwind, the overall picture is a description of what the fleeing Israelites encountered at the Red Sea. This is the great Old Testament demonstration of God's care for His people.

2. God's way was not clear to either Moses or the people as they huddled on the shore of the sea. What God would do was as mysterious as the waters of the sea, and what He did was make a way in the sea—to the complete surprise of the people. Deliverance from the sea and from Pharaoh came in and through the sea.

3. It can be exceedingly frustrating to remain in the dark about what God intends or works. But it is good to remember that God's way of doing surprising and unexpected

things means that, when we are in dire straits, we can still rest confidently in the assurance that our wonder-working, unpredictable God is yet working His plan for our benefit.

4. The waters of the Red Sea saved God's people, Israel. The waters of Holy Baptism save God's new Israel, God's chosen people, the Church.

5. You may not know every detail, or even any detail, about the way that God has planned for you, but you know enough! In the waters (the sea!) of Baptism, you know who you are, and in the Word, you know the shape of the life that God wants you to live. So, go live it, and watch as God opens the waters in surprising ways, revealing paths you would never have expected.

1. Was the past week one marked with a "day of trouble"? Tell the group about the greatest difficulty you faced this week.

Each of us face different challenges that, for us and at the time, are sufficient to cause pain and difficulty. It is good to remember that while one man's experience may seem inconsequential to others, to the one living through it, it can be quite significant. It is important, then, to value and take seriously every experience—even those that might seem "lightweight."

2. The psalmist says an odd thing in verse 3: that when he remembers God, he is disturbed. How can this be? Shouldn't remembering God bring joy and hope?

Apparently, thinking about God only served as a pointed reminder that God was not acting on his behalf at the present. It is possible that remembering past actions of God can discourage us when we wonder why He is not doing something similar in the present.

3. An inability to sleep is a typical corollary of trying times. The psalmist blames his insomnia on God (v. 4). Is this evidence of great faith or proof of little faith?

The psalmist clearly understands the hand of God active even in his struggle— that hand was actually holding his eyelids open! While those with little faith may well angrily blame God for their trouble, people of great faith may simply be acknowledging God's sovereignty and control as they strive to wait patiently for God's intervention and resolution of the problem.

4. The psalmist seems to engage in a healthy amount of reflection and meditation. What things get in the way of Christians emulating this practice of careful reflection and meditation?

It is clear from Scripture that meditation was a standard part of life for many of God's followers—though it must be admitted that this practice does not appear in the accounts of all the great biblical fathers of faith. Perhaps in our day, we associate meditation too much with Eastern religions and self-help gurus. Or perhaps, in typical masculine fashion, we would rather do something (anything!) other than sit and meditate. Truth be told, the discipline of meditation does not come easily to most men, and it requires an intentional commitment and relentless practice.

5. What sort of things should a person think about when he is meditating? What's the difference between meditating and "thinking hard"? Are there any dangers in devoting significant time to meditation?

Meditation is not magic, and there is no prescribed formula that describes its practice. In many ways, it is simply thinking hard, or thinking in a focused way. It has about it elements of study, prayer, and praise. It is a discipline that, in the case of this psalm, serves as a viable weapon against despair and hopelessness. With all of its benefits, it could run the risk of promoting passivity and inaction, and when the mind is allowed to set the agenda, it may actually foster greater angst and fear or reinforce wrong thinking. Good meditation must be informed and guided by God's truth—rehearsing God's saving actions is a safe guide.

6. Asaph fires off some rather pointed and perhaps even irreverent questions. What's the difference between these questions and the sort of questions asked by antagonistic unbelievers? Are there any questions that a believer should not ask God, even rhetorically?

It is a cherished notion that any question is a good question and that a believer should be able to tell God everything and ask God anything. The critical factor, of course, is faith. When faith is struggling, then the questions can be asked—they are asked in the sure knowledge of God's grace and provision. The unbeliever asks in derision and mocking, not from a heart that is breaking and looking to God for aid. This being said, a line of questioning can be pushed too far, and there comes a time (not readily defined or universally recognizable) when the creature must bow humbly and silently before his Creator and simply trust without demanding answers. To push beyond this limit is to push into unbelief and sin.

7. In verse 13, Asaph reminds us that God's way is holy. What does an emphasis on God's holy ways help us understand about God's way of doing things?

Not only does holiness point to the moral superiority of God's actions, but it also reminds us that God doesn't do things the way that we or other people do them. He is "wholly-other." He's unlike anything else that is. To emphasize God's holiness is to force us to recall that God's ways of doing things might not fit with what we expect—surely this is particularly evident at Calvary.

8. Why is a historical review of God's saving work (vv. 10–20) of such value to the psalmist in dealing with his difficult situation? What can the Church do to help its people to be better equipped to do the kind of remembering that Asaph finds so helpful?

Remembering what God has done instills confidence that God can and will do the same sort of thing again in the present—this time for me! It is important that the church recognizes the value of such remembering and cultivates this ability in its people by doing this remembering as part of the Divine Service. This occurs in the Scripture readings, in the sermon, and even in the liturgy that celebrates in careful language the history of God's saving work. The church that minimizes or eliminates any of these leaves its people with emaciated memories and feeble resources for battling the trials that come.

9. The struggle of Asaph seems to be quite personal, yet he finds hope and comfort by recalling God's actions for the whole people of Israel. What role does the Church (God's flock) play in an individual Christian's wrestling with life?

Asaph knows what many twenty-first-century Christians seems to have forgotten: we do not live in splendid isolation, cut off from the rest of the Church. In fact, it is good to remember that it is within and through the community of the Church in our local congregation that God works in our lives individually. Most Christians would reap immediate and great benefits simply by taking more seriously the importance of the Church as the place where God delivers His grace and gifts.

10. The psalm provides a great defense and example of the value that remembering has in the life of a believer. What are some of the significant memories that your group would include in a compilation of "holy events" that demonstrate God's faithfulness to His people as He fulfills His promise to save?

This list should certainly include the great moments of salvation history as recounted in the pages of the Bible. But, the compilation should not overlook contemporary events from the life of the group—times when God's mercy and grace were particularly in evidence. Retelling and remembering the story of God's faithfulness is an important part of the work of the Church and its people.

Week Four, Psalm 80
DAILY STUDY QUESTIONS

Monday Psalm 80:1–3

1. Familiarity with sheep may breed a certain fondness for the animals, but it does also confirm the fact that sheep have more than a few negative characteristics—stubbornness and stupidity ranking high on that list. Perhaps acknowledging the rightness of the designation as a sheep is merely an assent to the truth, harsh though it may be.

2. The cherubim were the two angelic beings with outspread wings that adorned the cover of the ark of the covenant. It was understood throughout the Old Testament corpus that God's earthly dwelling place was above or between the wings of those cherubim. So here Asaph is calling attention to the fact that God dwells with His people in power and majesty.

3. Either picture can communicate a sense of hope and confidence in God's intimate care and powerful capacity to save.

4. We all know that the same face can exude love and assurance or anger and disgust—indeed, the same face can communicate acceptance and affirmation or rejection and indifference. That God's face shines on us is the highest blessing available to man. Not a curse or, even worse, dismissive apathy, but rather delight and fondness is the message that God sends when He turns His face toward us.

5. Your present state of affairs will have much to do with your answers to these questions. Those struggling to know God's direction likely don't see much shepherding, while those struggling through a hard valley may not see much light shining from God's direction. To admit both the current situation and one's response to that situation is the beginning of finding a God-pleasing perspective on the situation.

Tuesday Psalm 80:4–7

1. Asaph is likely drawing what he thinks is a reasonable conclusion based on the evidence. The people are praying, nothing is happening; therefore, God must be angry with the prayer and refusing to answer. In fact, the idea of God being angry with a believer's prayer probably strikes most Christians as odd at best and as blasphemous at worst—God wouldn't do *that!* . . . would He?

2. Such physiological responses to trying times seem more common among the fairer sex, but given a situation severe and painful enough, it is conceivable that even

men will be overcome by tears and perhaps even see their appetite supplanted by a diet of tears. Clearly, such trials are the most severe sorts of loss and pain experienced in the course of life, and not the mundane "disappoints" that litter our daily lives.

3. Obviously, and distressingly, Asaph lays the blame at the feet of God. He is the one preparing the diet of tears and making the people the butt of ethnic and religious jokes throughout the region. This is bold faith—and well-placed faith—that rightly recognizes the author of suffering as the only one who can intervene to do something about the suffering.

4. Even Christians have enemies—or at least they have people around them who would love to see them discredited and disgraced. More accurately, the enemies of Christians want to see God brought low and ridiculed; unable to accomplish this feat, they settle for attacking God's people. The greatest delight of the antagonistic unbeliever is to see Christians made foolish by God's apparent inaction. When Christians enjoy no special perquisites, the enemy unbeliever assumes the vindication of his own unfaith.

5. "God of hosts" has nothing to do with domestic responsibilities or even the restaurant business. "Hosts" is a reference to God's warrior hosts. God of armies is a fair translation. The reminder that God has at His disposal armies of warriors is a reminder that He is more than able to plan and accomplish the saving of His people.

Wednesday Psalm 80:8–13

1. Many, this writer included, take great delight in watching things grow and prosper—especially when they have had a hand in the planting and nurturing of the plant. Perhaps there is some ancient bond with the earth that is still at work for us in a way that it was for Adam, who was made from the earth.

2. A vine is dependent on outside sustenance for its life and will produce nothing without this support. With it, however, the vine produces a precious and beautiful crop.

3. The vine was starting to grow in dramatic ways—stretching its canopy above the mountains of Canaan, from the Mediterranean to the Euphrates (a small empire realized under the reign of Solomon). But then Israel's fortunes turned sour, and it seemed that every unruly and ruthless superpower ("boar from the forest"), starting with Assyria, would pillage Israel every time they marched through the land on their way to another conquest. Israel had become easy pickings for anyone who happened along—cause for lament, indeed.

4. Asaph understands the right relation between creature and Creator. Creatures depend on their Creator for everything. So, God gathers His vine and plants it in Ca-

naan, and then that same God—for reasons that confound Asaph—breaks down the vineyard hedges and exposes His people to plundering and ignominy. Asaph knows who God is and what God does—only this God can help Israel.

5. Christians send their tender roots down into the fertile soil of God's own Word. By hearing, memorizing, meditating upon, and telling that Word—by participating in the Means of Grace—Christians put their roots where they belong and grow steadily in God's grace.

Thursday Psalm 80:14–18

1. It is clear that the psalmist recognizes his position of powerlessness. He needs God to step in and do what he is completely unable to do. It is also interesting that Asaph asks God simply to turn and look. The assumption (as that of a child appealing to a parent: "Dad, look!") is that when God sees the need, then God *will* intervene on behalf of His chosen vine. His compassion will compel Him to act. The child and the psalmist both count on that.

2. This, of course, is *the* great question that divides Christians from other interpreters—including Jewish interpreters. Christians cannot read this passage without thinking, "Jesus! He's talking about Jesus!" Others, though, would contend that the son is simply the nation of Israel. Perhaps the best answer recognizes both truths. Yes, the son is God's chosen people, but ultimately these people need one to accomplish what they cannot, and so the Son comes and, as Israel-reduced-to-one, fulfills the role and responsibilities of sonship and receives the blessing of God. In turn, He extends this blessing to His siblings through faith, to the whole people of God.

3. This is the literal realization of the old phrase "If looks could kill…" In the case of God, His look of rebuke does exactly that—it kills. A look of condemnation is sufficient to finish off those who live dependent on God's mercy.

4. The realization that God is working His plan by supplying His chosen Redeemer, who will serve as His instrument of rescue and restoration, should be a source of encouragement to those who have been laid low or wiped out by the realities of life. That God provides and strengthens this Son is proof of His ability and willingness to step in on behalf of His suffering people.

5. Asaph was not afraid to demand the promised Savior who would redeem the people who had been cut down by the nations around. He prayed with zeal and conviction borne of vibrant faith in God's character and promise. Perhaps too many Christians' prayers reflect a hesitance and timidity unworthy of our faith and our God.

Friday Psalm 80:19

1. Though we are each unique individuals with our unique ways of handling life's situations, we share a common propensity to insist on finding our own way, so it is likely that you can recall a time when you preferred hanging on to your rope over letting go and falling into God's mercy.

2. The sticking problem—the thing that keeps us clinging to our failed efforts, hollow excuses, and discredited plans is, quite simply and powerfully, pride. Unwilling to admit defeat, we would often rather fail under our own power than admit inability and helplessness that needs God's intervention. Self-reliance and self-preservation (at the least, the preservation of a modicum of self-respect and dignity) demand that one not quit trying, that one not admit abject helplessness.

3. This likely occurs on a regular basis, often under the guise of "sincere faith." Truth be told, humans would rather use God as a tool in their arsenal of resources for getting through life rather than as the reason for life. Too often, even believers confuse a dignified and orderly "seeking God's help" with the desolate and desperate cry of faith. This is the difference between seeking to enlist God's aid in the project *you* are doing and wailing in utter hopelessness as you willingly and unheedingly admit complete helplessness and pathetic dependence. Such radical humility is the hallmark of Christian faith, but perhaps it is not a common mark in the Church today.

4. Christianity is not for individuals. Christianity is about the community. It is about the Church. We never exist in isolation. Our faith is not about "me and Jesus." It is always about Christ and His Church. So Asaph rightly prays as a member of that corporate Body. So should you pray as a member of Christ's Body, and specifically plead to God for what His Church (as present in your congregation and more widely in the entire world) actually needs.

5. A great place to begin is with confession. Start by enumerating your failures and by acknowledging to God your crushing failure and your continued and complete need for His mercy and grace. Offer this prayer again, several times throughout the day, to recenter your life on the only sure foundation—God and His grace given in Christ.

Week Four, Psalm 80
GROUP BIBLE STUDY
(Questions are on pp. 120–21.)

1. Have you ever heard a prayer that sounded more like a sermon? What's the right balance between keeping a prayer succinct and direct and pouring out a poetic exhortation that recounts most of the highlights of salvation history?

In contemporary Western culture, *short, heartfelt,* and perhaps even *nonintellectual* seem to be the desired adjectives when it comes to our prayers. Yet, the psalms (including this one) offer many examples of fervent prayers that are not only heartfelt and passionate but are also rich with the truth of God's saving activity. In other words, a paucity or deficiency of doctrinal or historical depth should not be considered a virtue in one's prayer life!

2. Scripture likes the image of God's people as a flock of sheep. In what specific ways does this seem an apt description? What changes might be needed if the Church were to adopt this understanding of its own identity and purpose?

The potential applications of the sheep metaphor are vast: Sheep are stubborn. Sheep function with a herd mentality. Sheep need a strong leader they can trust. Sheep are prone to ignore their circumstances and wander into trouble. Sheep are not always particularly pleasant. Sheep make a lot of noise when they are afraid or unhappy. The list could easily continue. If our churches were to take seriously the nature of people as sheep, and would accept the need to guide and care for the flock (rather than manage or simply organize it), perhaps our church's servants would be more assertive and intentional about the leadership and teaching they supply. Of course, your group may have other thoughts about what it takes to care for a flock of sheep.

3. Does God need to be persuaded to save? What's the value (or perhaps even the point!) in the psalmist's appeal to God to put some of His power into action on behalf of His people?

This is the timeless question about prayer: if God does what God does—and saving His people is one of the things that He does—then why bother trying to motivate Him to action for the sake of His people? Besides, who am *I* to tell *God* what to do? The beauty of prayer, as demonstrated here by Asaph, is that it recognizes God as the source of hope and promise. It is profound praise as the one who prays acknowledges God's place as Lord and as the one and only one who can intervene with His power to save. Prayer helps us order our priorities and keeps us looking in the right direction for our longed-for deliverance. Prayer, even—especially—a demand for divine action, is faith in action.

4. Notice the pronouns of the psalm—especially in the first seven verses. What is conspicuous by its absence? What conclusions might be reached on the basis of the concern of Asaph and the way that he approaches the problem?

In our Western, especially American, context, it is jarring to realize that Asaph never uses a singular, first-person pronoun. Every first-person pronoun is plural. Asaph understands that it is the community of God that matters. He is concerned about a trial that affects the whole community, and he prays for the deliverance of all that community. For Asaph, faith has nothing to do with self-fulfillment, individual needs, or a "personal relationship" with God. Asaph is rightly focused on what God is doing in and with the entire community of believers. He understands that his place is within that community. Explore as a group the degree to which our churches have become more concerned with the individual than with the community and the ways that this impacts the Church's life, mission, and witness.

5. Where do you hear the laughter of the Church's enemies? What can or should the Church do about this?

The arena of "science" (especially evolutionary science) is a fertile ground for generating laughter at the expense of believers. So, too, is the hypocrisy readily seen by observers of those who claim faith. Derision by the enemies of God and His Church is not to be escaped; it is to be expected. The absence of such attack is cause for serious introspection and evaluation of the degree of a church's faithfulness to the call of Christ.

6. In what sense is the image of God's people as a grapevine a heightening of the point that the people are dependent on their God for everything? Which image—sheep or vine—do you find most compelling?

Sheep are able, at least, to forage for themselves and to flee from danger. A vine has neither of those options, depending on the provision of all that it needs to be given to it, and counting on others to provide protection. The radical dependence of creatures is not a truth that is often given much consideration in the twenty-first century. It has a way of diminishing the self-importance and self-preservation myths that have become so critical to our Western way of life. Sheep or vine is not much of a choice—either leaves you with the realization that we creatures are more dependent and helpless than we care to admit.

7. The psalmist describes the tremendous vitality and "success" of the vine as it spread and covered the land (vv. 8–11). Yet God obviously had a different vision for His chosen vine, allowing it to be pillaged by every enemy who came along. What is God's definition of success? How does it jibe with most of our definitions of success?

What man calls success (in Psalm 80, a strong and influential nation-state), God apparently dismisses as insignificant. That allowing His vine to be molested and diminished fits with His plan for His vine teaches that God does not operate with our understandings of success. For God, success is always about His plan for His creation being accomplished. Ultimately, this means the creation acting like creatures, and a healthy dose of humility is always necessary for this outcome! Indeed, affliction was part of the plan and contributed to what God deemed a success for His vine. That Asaph did not fully grasp this reminds us of what a challenge it is for creatures to come to terms with God's sort of success.

8. The psalm takes many human attributes and applies them to God. How many can your group identify? Do you think this procedure helps or hurts our understanding of God's nature and being?

The application of a human characteristic to God is called an anthropomorphism. Applying human emotions to God is an anthropopathism. The psalm has many examples of each: God's hand, face, eyes, ears, and anger over wrong prayers. It is a fair discussion, whether attributing human characteristics to God might mislead people into thinking of God in too familiar a way and thus forgetting the fact that He is "wholly other" and altogether transcendent. On the other hand, we can only know God by analogy, and thinking of Him in human terms may be the only way we can begin to grasp His reality.

9. What's the difference between calling on the LORD's (Yahweh's) name for help (v. 18) and simply looking heavenward and asking for help?

It is important to remember that not every prayer is a prayer of faith; that is, not every prayer is directed to the only God that is and asked in faith. While it might seem that, if someone is praying, then he is obviously praying to the only God that actually exists, if that pray-er does not acknowledge the triune God who has revealed Himself in His Son, Jesus, then that person's prayer—regardless how heartfelt and sincere—is actually directed into mere thin air or, worse, to a false god, an idol. (See 1 Corinthians 10:19–20 and John 14:13–14, our Lord's instruction that prayer must be done in His name.)

10. What is the right relationship between complete reliance on God's necessary provision (as expressed throughout the psalm and especially in v. 19), and working hard with all your might and available resources to accomplish the same thing for which you pray?

Strange as it seems, these are not mutually exclusive options. In fact, God's Word makes it clear that they coexist—indeed, in the life of a believer, both are simultaneously present and both are working at full strength. Even as we rely on God for *everything*, we work with all our might to try to accomplish *everything*. This is the lively and powerful dynamic of the Christian faith.

Week Five, Psalm 83
Daily Study Questions

Monday Psalm 83:1–4

1. Knowing that silence is golden and acting on that knowledge are vastly different things, of course. It seems that men sometimes struggle with knowing when it is wise to speak and when it is wise to remain silent—or at least members of the opposite sex have been known to level such charges against men.

2. The text presents us with three voices: there is the voice of the psalmist, who is offering his pious prayer; there is the uproarious voice of Israel's enemies, who plot against and threaten God's people; and there is the voice of God—distressingly silent.

3. The enemies of God are succumbing to an old trap of multiplying their guilt by multiplying their words. Often, the wisest path is that of restraint and reticence in speaking. In the case of these verses, the speaking being done by the enemies is confirming their sin and magnifying their guilt (Proverbs 10:19).

4. Though all things might seem to be arrayed against them, in their favor they have the fact of their own identity: they are God's people, His treasured possession. To be so favored by the God of the universe effectively eclipses every other experienced reality. Even the silence of God is given a new interpretation when seen in the perspective of God's promises—the silence is not forever.

5. You have the same assurance that Israel had: God is your God and you are His people, and this is a reality accomplished at God's initiative by means of His promise. The Gospel as it comes to you in Word and Sacrament guarantees that you are God's child and that you have nothing to fear from the threats that surround you.

Tuesday Psalm 83:5–8

1. Likely, the forces at work against you are not the names of nations or tribes but the names of worries, responsibilities, mistakes, afflictions, or even people who are making your life more challenging than you would choose it to be.

2. Almost every experience in life has a spiritual component—whether these are threats that undermine faith or catalysts for growth depends on how these experiences are met and handled. Indeed, the source of our challenges is of little consequence. What is important is that each one is met from the perspective of faith. Real challenges can be met with the real grace and strength of God's promises.

3. Whether all of these tribes actually gathered to form an alliance of conspiracy

against Israel is not the point. The point is that Asaph and Israel felt the threat as if it was an all-out conspiracy against the Lord God and His people. The motive is simple and operative yet today: hatred of God and of anything to do with God.

4. It is explicit in verse 5: Asaph acknowledges that the nations' conspiracy is aimed against God. Israel is only incidental—so it is with Christians today.

5. Understanding that the forces arrayed against God and His truth will frequently vent their anger and hatred against God's people can help the believer develop a new appreciation for the challenges that he experiences from day to day—especially the challenges that arise from those who qualify as enemies of God's truth.

Wednesday Psalm 83:9–12

1. Rivalries can extend beyond the arena of sports into any form of competition: workplace, romance, academics, and neighborhood one-upmanship. For most men, rivalries do not go away with adulthood!

2. It is interesting how easily feelings of animosity toward a "rival" can become feelings of respect and even fondness when some greater rival appears, one that threatens both you and your old rival. The truth is that rivals frequently share a remarkable number of common characteristics. Whether healed by marriage or a common cause, it is not surprising that old rivals can suddenly and enduringly become fast friends.

3. The key to appreciating the import of the psalm is to recognize much more than a regional rivalry at work in the animosity between Israel and her neighbors. While there are many who would like to reduce all human conflict to mere rivalry—the crosstown sort that serves to bind those of a community into a common cause and emotion—Scripture is clear that there are people who are genuine enemies of God. While this is hard for us to accept, there are those who choose to live at odds with God and His truth, those who choose to reject God and God's people. These are the enemies that are in sight for Asaph. He is dealing with spiritual warfare that transcends the sort of petty rivalries that are so familiar to us. These threatening enemies are plotting to take "the pastures of *God*" (v. 12).

4. A reasonable test might be whether the "someone" is trying to kill you—but that is not really the point. The only issue that matters is where your enemy stands with God. On the Last Day, the only criteria that will matter will be one's relationship with God, and on that day even those who had seemed friendly enough may well be revealed as enemies of the Gospel and God's truth. This is part of the practice of living with spiritual eyes that learn to see what God sees.

5. The discipline of prayer is best learned in the time of immediate need—pray

for those rivals and enemies who come to mind, and do it *now*.

Thursday Psalm 83:13–16

1. Men have a tendency to fall victim to their own desire to fix things. It's worth remembering (small solace, perhaps) that God wired this desire into the male sex, and that more times than not, it works for the good of others. Still, there are definite limits to what a man—even one in shining armor—can accomplish; that, of course, is precisely the point.

2. Of course, this is a false dichotomy. One needn't choose between the two but should actually pursue both simultaneously. It is always time for both. The follower of God is never exempt from his responsibility to work for the good of others and to use every available resource in the effort. At the same time—indeed, at the exact same time—the Christian man fully knows that he is utterly dependent on God and His merciful intervention for any hope of success in any situation. Human responsibility coupled with God's perfect plan and activity is always the lively dynamic in which we live and act.

3. The wind, the fire, and the storm are all instruments in God's plan. They do God's bidding and serve His purposes. It is tempting to think that creation is wild, reckless, and arbitrary, but Asaph sees it rightly: all things in creation do God's bidding and work according to His purposes.

4. Perhaps a more robust and forthright admission of the divine component of natural disasters would increase both human humility and hope in the face of the "random" intrusions of the natural world. To admit God's purposes at work even in life's tragedies may help us better respond in confident faith, rather than in anger or despair. It may be wise to reclaim that old but accurate phrase, "an act of God," to describe natural events that defy human control.

5. At the end of verse 16, Asaph injects what might be a surprising twist in this otherwise strident and rather nasty prayer against God's enemies. When all is said and done, and God has heeded the prayer and sternly rebuked the rebellious nations, Asaph's hope is these rebellious people will repent and turn to God. In other words, he is not vindictively praying for the destruction of these enemies, but for their conversion. He wants the enemy to be swallowed not in God's consuming wrath, but in God's enduring forgiveness and grace. Yet Asaph realizes that this sort of repentance can only follow the harshest action of the Law—thus the content of his prayer.

Friday Psalm 83:17–18

1. There is no shortage of sin and evil at work in this world that could lead a

righteous man to yearn for justice and could even spark in him a desire for revenge against the wrong. The yearning for wrongs to be righted, for justice, is rooted in the Law planted inside each man by the Creator.

2. While we may feel justified in our desire for vengeance, the psalmist gives no evidence that this drives him. Indeed, the text makes clear that Asaph's desire is actually that the sinners may come to acknowledge the lordship of the only mighty God.

3. As James reminds us (James 2:19), recognizing God's existence and even His sovereignty is a far cry from yielding to His rule and receiving His grace in humble faith. The latter eventuates in the eternal inheritance prepared for God's people, the former is the inescapable confession of all creatures on the Last Day—even those who are condemned to everlasting sorrow and suffering in hell.

4. The God who alone is the Sovereign Lord of all creation—the only God that is—has a specific identity: He is the Lord, that is, He is Yahweh—the God of Abraham, Isaac, and Jacob—the God of Jesus. God is not a generic force or an idea plastic enough to be forced into whatever mold any given religion can think of. God is God, and this God is revealed in His actions in history on behalf of His people, Israel and the new Israel, the Church. Those who refuse to confess this specificity of God are, by definition, worshiping a false god—an idol.

5. While He *is our* God, He is also the God of all creation—He has no rivals; there are no opposing forces with which He must battle; there are no people or parts of His creation that lie outside His jurisdiction—He is Lord of all. This has the potential to foster a great deal of confidence in God's people—as well as a renewed hope in the ability of God to fulfill every promise.

Week Five, Psalm 83
GROUP BIBLE STUDY
(Questions are on pp. 146–47.)

1. Describe a time in your life (maybe from childhood or perhaps just recently) when you had to deal with a bully. How did you handle it? How did it turn out?

It seems that the world is starting to pay more attention to the reality of bullies and the real grief they generate in the lives of many—especially children. In your discussion, pay special attention to the number of these bully situations that were resolved by an appeal to a higher authority, such as a parent or teacher.

2. Asaph is quite specific and perhaps even abrupt in his appeal (some might say demand) for God to do something about the loud and dangerous enemies who are threatening His people. How does this prayer fit with the typical prayer, "if it be Your will," so regularly heard today? Would Asaph's prayer be better if it included the phrase "according to God's will"?

True prayer may not always bother with the niceties of formula and pious packaging —there may be no time or, as in the case here, there may be no need. It is worth remembering that every prayer of faith is offered with the implicit understanding that God's will is paramount and must be done—indeed, the believer desires nothing less. Nevertheless, rigidly and ritually reciting the necessary verbiage ("If it be Your will" or some form thereof) may actually blunt the urgency of a prayer or dissuade believers from a heartfelt expression of their real needs and desires. Prayer should be a genuine conversation with the Creator—at times of great need, it may be quite pointed and thoughtlessly visceral. This is a mark not of bad theology or immature faith, but the opposite.

3. Millennia old, the evil intent voiced in verse 4 sounds thoroughly and eerily contemporary. Does this verse serve only to highlight the rabid anti-Semitism that has been a sad (indeed, too often horrific) and recurrent theme in world history, or might a more considered interpretation of the verse contain even richer and more relevant spiritual truth?

It requires little effort to imagine reading the same words on an "anti-Israel" Web site, or on a protest poster brandished in a city of the Near East. While one should recognize and confess the fact of virulent and devastating anti-Semitism that has marred the actions of Western nations and even the Western Church, it is also important to see in verse 4 the spiritual component. Israel is best understood not simply as a nation-state or a cultural group or even a particular race. From a biblical view, Israel is best understood as the chosen people of God—a designation now best applicable to God's Church. This hatred and conflict has its roots in Genesis 3:15.

4. The psalmist's list of tribes and peoples that were arrayed against Israel reads like a veritable rogues gallery of ancient Fertile-Crescent bullies. Why was this threat about more than politics?

If Asaph had stood on the temple mount in Jerusalem and looked far enough in a circle around himself, he would have been looking into each threatening nation or tribe listed in the psalm, with the final greatest threat, Asshur [Assyria], off in the far distance to the east, completing the "circle of fear." These nations were not worshiping Yahweh, and so the threat and the conflict were never merely about politics or culture, but were ultimately an issue of spiritual truth—theology.

5. Is Asaph simply suffering from a persecution complex? Is there reason for Christians today to be concerned about the threats that encompass them, or would that be succumbing to unfounded paranoia?

"Just because you're paranoid, it doesn't mean that they *aren't* out to get you." A very '70s-style poster proclaiming this wisdom, or something close to it, once graced a band-room wall in a Michigan high school. The point is actually true and deserves some attention. Perhaps God's enemies *are* a threat to us. The alarm and plea of Asaph are not the result of an active imagination or simple paranoia. In fact, the nations surrounding Israel were quite determined to reduce Israel to insignificance or nonexistence. While it is not helpful to live in paranoia—seeing enemies where none exist—it is equally dangerous to deny a threat that is real. The threat of God's enemies against God's people is quite real.

6. When Asaph considers the threats that surround Israel, he prays for the kind of intervention that had brought low Israel's enemies in centuries long past. How does the recollection of old victories bring comfort in the present? What are some old memories you can use to bring you encouragement during new trials?

Asaph has in mind two great victories from the times of the Judges: Gideon's rout of Midian and its kings (Judges 7–8) and the victory of Deborah and Barak (Judges 4). To recognize God's past faithfulness serves as a catalyst to renewed hope during present difficulties and crises—if God did it then, He can do it again! It is a good idea to develop a sort of memory bank of God's past faithfulness, one that includes not only great events from the Bible but also great events of mercy and deliverance from your own life. Start with the baptismal font . . .

7. Consider the psalmist's chosen examples of Israel's past victories (Judges 4 and 7–8). What do these two stories have in common? What point does the psalmist make by choosing these stories?

The story of Deborah goes out of it way to stress that the victory belonged to a woman, and the story of Gideon is marvelous because the victory is won by a puny "army" of three hundred men. In both instances, it was clear (at least to Asaph and his readers) that it was not the human component that assured the victory but only God's intervention. Out of the weakest of human "champions," God was able to achieve His plan and give victory to His people. With history like this, Israel can rest assured that God is more than able to meet every need with even the feeblest human resources.

8. How does the imprecatory prayer of Asaph (longing to see his neighbors reduced to dung; v. 10) square with our Lord's command to love our enemies (Matthew 5:43–47)?

This is one of the especially thorny questions that demands an answer whenever reading the psalms of lament that so readily slide into the category known as imprecatory psalms. While it is tempting (and easiest) to ignore the question, it is not one that threatens our faith or even the consistency of God's Word. Even as Christians, we live in a double-bind: we must pray for our enemies and even seek to love them—they are fellow creatures for whom our Lord died and the object of God's love. But we must also yearn for God's justice to extend into the whole universe—which means the defeat and destruction of those who oppose Him. In other words, I can love my enemy—those who are eager to see *my* downfall and humiliation—even while I pray for God to strike down all who thwart His justice and deny His truth. When this comes to pass, there is rejoicing at God's promised restoration—setting right all that has been wrong and bringing justice to all corners of this world. But there is also sorrow that those we have learned to love have cut themselves off from God's mercy. Even in the New Testament, it continues to be both things (Luke 19:27; 20:16).

9. In verse 17, Asaph drives home the sharp point of his prayer for the Lord's wrath to be unleashed on Israel's enemies, pleading that they may "be put to shame and dismayed forever . . . [to] perish in disgrace." Yet, in the very next verse, he indicates that he offers this harsh petition only as a means to his final desire: that these enemies "may know that You alone . . . are the Most High." How can those who perish know the Lord? How might you reconcile these two verses?

There are at least two possible answers to the problem posed by the juxtaposition of the verses. The first is to note that the psalmist doesn't actually pray for the conversion of these enemies but only for their forced confession of God's identity. This is not too different from what St. Paul writes in Philippians 2:10 or St. John in Revelation 1:7. Killing and then making alive is the work of God through preaching. We are brought low, we are killed, and then through faith in Christ, we are made alive. One could read Asaph's words as an appeal for God to bring the enemies to nothing so that they may be raised in faith.

10. How will your increased understanding of the spiritual war being waged on the battleground called earth shape the way that you think, act, speak, and pray in the coming week? What do those around you need from you if you are faithfully to witness God's truth about this spiritual conflict?

Ideally, participants in the study should have a heightened awareness of the spiritual realities that attend all the actions, interactions, and communications that make up our daily lives. It takes training and practice, but the Christian should strive to see all of life with the eyes of faith, recognizing the spiritual component that impacts even the most routine and "secular" events and conversations that make up our lives. Is your conversation partner a fellow believer? Or is he, in fact, an enemy of the Gospel—one who needs your prayer and your witness?

Week Six, Psalm 90
Daily Study Questions

Monday Psalm 90:1–2

1. Given our mobile society and the transitory nature of our lives, perhaps the longest you've lived in one place is only a few years. Along with long-time friends and familiar surroundings, another good that comes with longevity in a home or at least a community, is the comfort and security of what is familiar.

2. *Abide* is a particularly apt word for the way that we remain in God as we live in the many different places of this world. We abide in God by contemplating His truth, cultivating His way of seeing life, communing with Him in the Means of Grace, and committing ourselves to following His way of living. We dwell in God always and concentrate our efforts on ensuring that the generation that follows us does the same.

3. Certainly, the psalm begins with the greatest of comfort: God has been our dwelling place, our refuge, and we have reaped enormous blessings of peace and security from having so great a dwelling in this world. The grandeur conveyed in verse 2 reinforces our sense of security by stressing the power and majesty of the God in whom we dwell. He is able to provide the safe dwelling we need.

4. Moses wants to confront the reader with the radical difference between the Creator and His creation. As permanent and solid as we consider the mountains and the earth itself to be, next to God even these "certainties" appear insubstantial and ephemeral. Before there is a world, there is God. After the earth has made its final deliberate circuit around the sun, there is God. Mountains and (to an impossibly greater degree) people are mere blips in time and space next to the everlasting God.

5. Maybe it will mean taking a few minutes during your lunch hour to pray about your dwelling place. Perhaps you can write the first verse of the psalm on a note card or business card and put it in a prominent place where your eyes will fall on it repeatedly through the day (your car's dashboard or your computer keyboard or in your front pocket could be good choices).

Tuesday Psalm 90:3–6

1. Certainly, God's creation of man out of the dust, and the subsequent curse that sinful man would be forced to return to the dust, is in mind here—the emphasis being on man's fallibility, temporality, and, ultimately, his corruptibility. The same points are made with emphasis with the imposition of ashes at the beginning of Lent.

2. The psalmist makes it uncomfortably clear that it is God who is behind the horrible reality of death. *He* turns man back to dust. *He* pronounces the terrible judgment: "Return; back to the dust with you!"

3. Christians know this truth and, following 2 Peter 2:9, typically use it to reassure and encourage downtrodden and discouraged believers. Moses, however, uses the same concept to convict and humble his readers. This is an outstanding example of the way that the same words can convey either Law or Gospel, depending entirely on the context in which they are spoken and heard.

4. A flood comes suddenly, powerfully. It is impossible to stand against it. It is indiscriminate, wiping out everything in its path. And, when it passes, it leaves devastation and grief in its wake. Death as a flood is an apt image, indeed.

5. While it is impossible to know the precise motive of Moses for penning these verses, it seems clear that his goal was not to lead his readers into a pit of depression. Even granting this possible result, the believer should not allow this to be the final word but should use the sober lesson as a impetus to renewed trust in God alone, who salvages human existence. For the Christian, life is not finally an absurd and bitter joke but a gift full of meaning and significance as it harmonizes with God's master plan.

Wednesday Psalm 90:7–10

1. In Romans 4:15, St. Paul rightly points out that "the law brings wrath." We don't like to be compelled to face our shortcomings and failings. So the message of these psalm verses is not a pleasant one. Worse, though, is the psalm's focus on the much more significant wrath that is provoked by sin and the Law's accusation: God's wrath.

2. We try to hide our sin that shames us from the purview of others—especially others that are important to us. This creates enormous barriers within our relationships and generates even more sin. Secrecy does not mitigate sin; it complicates it.

3. The attempt to keep our sins a secret is perhaps intended above all for the comfort of ourselves. We hide the truth from ourselves, which only results in self-deception and resistance to the only possible source of healing—repentance. To have your sins exposed is the greatest mercy imaginable—painful, yes; but mercy nonetheless. One does not repent of secret sins; they are, therefore, lethal.

4. In one sense, it's certainly true that no one knows the exact day, hour, or minute of death. Moses, though, might respond by saying something like this: "You know well enough your length of time: you've got seventy or maybe eighty years at the most." Even in the twenty-first century, we know that very few people get more than a decade past a

century of life. The real point is that we know that we do not have unlimited time to live, and whether it is 20 years or 110 years, it is always too little and too filled with sorrow and sighing. Moses want us to face the fact that death is inevitable, that even a "full" life is a short life that leaves you in the same place as the person who dies young.

5. Seventy or eighty years may seem like a very long time to a youth, but those who have already spent more than half of their allotment realize quickly that the time is short and must be lived in relation to God's truth if it is to have any meaning or significance. This is not a new thought, of course; the Romans had already made the truth proverbial: *tempus fugit, carpe diem*. It's not bad advice, even from the perspective of faith: time flies, so seize the day.

Thursday Psalm 90:11-12

1. It's important to remember that anger is not inherently sinful—a position that seems to find its way into thinking of Christians. At the same time, it is also true that we have a way of justifying anger that is plainly sinful—like punching walls out of our frustration. The only "good" anger is anger over sin, the kind of anger God aims at His sinful and rebellious creatures. Remember that Jesus was angry on more than one occasion but always for the same reason: sinful man was fighting God's plan.

2. Many young believers have memorized Luther's "What does this mean?" answers to each of the Ten Commandments and know that "We should fear and love God so that..." Unfortunately, many have also been taught that this fear really means respect or reverence, because Christians no longer have anything to fear before God. While it must be stressed with unrestrained emphasis that in Christ there is no condemnation for God's people, it is also true that God still hates sin and that our Lord urged His disciples to fear Him who can condemn body and soul to hell (Matthew 10:28)! Fear (as in cowering terror) still has an appropriate place, even in the life of a believer. Consider the reactions of Jesus' disciples when confronted with His divinity: Mark 4:35–41; Luke 5:4–10; and Revelation 1:17.

3. In verse 11, the psalmist asks a rhetorical question, and we know the answer: we don't get it. Swimming in sin day in and day out, and living in a world and in relationships that are awash in sin, we have a tendency to become calloused and even oblivious to the pervasiveness and perversion of sin that pollutes every moment of every part of our lives. God, on the other hand, is holy. He sees every sin and hates every sin. That any of us is allowed to continue breathing is a mark of astounding mercy on the part of God. While we may be complacent and comfortable with sin, God is not. So, what we deem unfair in life is better recognized as a small token of what we, by our sins rightly deserve.

God is not unfair, we just forget how truly horrible and damning our sins are.

4. "Your days are numbered" is ordinarily intended as a threat of an indication that death is imminent. The truth, though, is that this is the reality for everyone—even the infant only hours old. Whatever the "number" may be, it is certainly finite. Admitting the limit of life is the point here. There are probably many aspects of wisdom that are enhanced by a willingness to face the brevity and limit of life with honesty. Above all, one learns not to overestimate his own importance and not to forget what it means to be a creature living in absolute dependence on the mercy of the Creator. The wisest people are those who have the right perspective on life—they see it from God's perspective.

5. This question raises many other issues about the relationship between faith and works, and also the problem of sinful passivity or inaction on the part of Christians who are rightly relying on God's grace. The simplest (and therefore best?) answer is that human beings should strive to be what God made them to be, and wisdom is part of that picture. In other words, Christians want to have wise hearts because that is what God created them to do. Striving after wisdom is part of what it means to be human.

Friday Psalm 90:13-17

1. No, Moses is not bipolar (manic/depressive). He is living wisely and learning to see everything from God's perspective. As long as God is in control—and He is always in control—then it is possible for the believer to hope with joy, confident of God's mercy and ultimate provision. One does not have to choose between the two different messages. Both are true. Man is a passing shadow with no significance and, at the same time, God is in control and working all things according to His purpose, thus bringing meaning and significance to our lives. The reason for the wild swings in the psalm is the reality that defines our lives: we are sinners struggling in a broken world, and we are creatures destined for eternal joy in God's re-created world.

2. In verse 3, God's justice delivered the stern judgment on sinful man: Return to dust. Now in verse 13, God's redeemed creature uses the same word to exhort God to forsake His wrath and return to His people with mercy and compassion. This is the prayer of faith that clings to God's promise even when it is only righteous wrath that is being experienced.

3. The perceptive reader of the psalms (indeed of the entire Bible) has caught on to these questions: it is both all the time. This is the duality or the dynamic of life lived in God's truth. We know the reality of personal sin and failure and the subsequent wrath of God, and we know the reality of God's mercy and forgiveness and the consequent joy and hope that fills us and "all our days." It is always both at once.

4. Not content with an even balance sheet, Paul looks forward to overwhelming blessing and glory from God that will bury all the sorrow and suffering of this life in the eternal joy of God's promises fulfilled. This is the "work" that God is accomplishing and that Moses prays to see (v. 16). The final experience of God's grace and glory will overtake, eclipse, and at last eradicate all the agony of this present life.

5. The final mercy of God is that He does not make us wait to begin to see the importance and significance of our lives. Even now, He gives meaning to our living by using us and our vocations (our service to family, friends, neighbors, and total strangers) to fulfill His purposes in this world. It is His mercy that takes what we attempt through our feeble and meager efforts and confirms them as His own work. Through us, God works in this world. As St. Paul reminds us, our labor in the Lord is never in vain (1 Corinthians 15:58).

1. Under what circumstances do you feel especially small and insignificant next to the grandeur and immensity of the universe?

Most of us have experienced the overwhelming rush of the creation's size and wonder reducing our own person and existence to puny inconsequence. A star-filled, sky, a wild ocean with towering waves, or a cemetery with its pang of mortality and display of the utter insignificance of lives in a few brief centuries can all succeed in reducing us to a more humble—and accurate—assessment of our place within the universe.

2. What does the opening of the psalm (v. 2) teach us about the relationship between God and His creation?

More than simply a message of God's authority or power, the psalm makes it clear that God far surpasses His creation and that His existence is in no way dependent on the creation. All that exists derives entirely from Him. And before there was a world or any form of matter, there was God. The creation is utterly and thoroughly dependent on its Creator.

3. Think about the wider culture and then about the Church's culture; what evidence of man's effort to deny death's reality do you see in each? Why does Moses, with such zeal, drive home the point of man's mortality and futility?

Your group could probably spend the bulk of your meeting time discussing the culture's ceaseless attempts to deny or hide the reality of death. It is important to realize that even in the Church, where we should know better, people are often reluctant to face the fact of death—especially one's own death. For Moses, this is the point that must be acknowledged: man is small and insignificant—doomed to die. God is immortal and all-consuming.

4. Which of the metaphors for man's impermanence and insignificance (vv. 3–6) seems the most powerful or effective? What metaphors might a twenty-first-century psalmist use to convey the same message?

Dust, a night-watch, flotsam in a flood, or grass in the sun—all deliver a sobering message of the brevity, contingency, and futility of human life. Which is most potent has much to do with personal experience, which is one reason for the litany of images. The very structure of these verses—the collision of rapid-fire pictures of human meaninglessness—actually serves to convey the same message of the incoherence and out-of-control chaos that lies beneath the false veneer of calm and orderly life that we maintain in our daily interactions with one another. Encourage the group to think creatively about some contemporary images or metaphors that can help to dispel the pretensions that we use to hide the horrific reality about the futility of life apart from God.

5. The appalling tragedy of verse 6 is that what starts with such promise and even beauty so quickly disintegrates into death, decay, and nothingness. Is this pathetic perspective on life appropriate in a Christian worldview, or is this merely morbid and unworthy of the optimism that should define the lives of God's people?

This is the serious underlying question that can generate some fierce discussion. What place does such an unflinching and bleak assessment of the abject futility of human life have in a Christian's thinking? This picture is a far cry from the prosperity and joy that many Christians seem to assume as their entitlement for living righteously or for believing the right things. Indeed, this poignant and disquieting portrait of life's stupid pointlessness must be included in a Christian's worldview. To acknowledge this picture is to admit the final and complete failure of humanity's attempt to live life without God. No matter what, every life always ends in death, and every life always dissolves into insignificance and meaninglessness. No human philosophy, religion, or technology has or ever will overcome the inherent vanity and absurdity of human existence. Since the fall, this is the lot of us all. We are in desperate need of a savior. We need God. This is the point of the psalm, and this is the fundamental truth that must animate every faithful Christian life.

6. There is a reason for the emptiness and despair that are at the heart of every human life. How do verses 7 and 8 fit with the preceding verses? Why is it that the wrath of God seems to be so seldom mentioned (much less seriously considered), even in Christian churches?

Our lives end in tragic futility because we are sinners and God is just. It is that simple. Every human attempt to explain suffering in the world will never succeed if it does not simply admit the base problem of human sin—rebellion against God. Of course, the terror of sin is that God actually takes it seriously and deals with it with exacting and obliterating justice. Perhaps the ubiquity and commonality of sin makes it seem less important. "So you sinned? No big deal. It happens to all of us; nobody's perfect!" The truth, though, as the psalm so painfully and pitilessly impresses upon us, is that God thinks otherwise. He hates sin. He punishes sin. He damns sinners—every one of them, no exceptions.

7. Why is it that men like to fancy themselves in the role of a cowboy or swashbuckler who goes out with his boots on in a blaze of glory? How does the psalmist portray the end of life in verse 9? Which account is more accurate? Why do you think men are so inclined to recast the grim realities that attend death?

We do not go out like John Wayne, surrounded by flags, heroism, and glory. In the end, it all reduces to the same pathetic whimper. We can stand up in defiance, but death always gets the last word, and the final result is the same, regardless the circumstances or man's attempts at recasting it in shades of glory. Death is death. It is a relentless force that gets us all, reducing every man (even the hero) to dust and a fading memory. To face this truth is asking too much of most men, hence the myth of glory and honor in death. But Moses is right. It all ends with a feeble and faint whisper—a sigh, a whimper. Whatever we have done, however we have lived, it all comes to the same end, and there is nothing any man can do to alter the fact. This is the sick joke that lies at the center of every human life, haunting us and mocking our vain attempts to deny it. Admission of this truth has only one outcome: despair.

8. Overall, the psalmist presents a pointed and painfully frank assessment of the place and significance of man in the universe. While we may be forced grudgingly to admit the truth of what he presents, we may have doubts about what to do with the information. Should these hard truths be a prominent component of the Church's message? Should it be a regular theme in preaching, or is this one of those doctrines that is better left in the textbooks and not openly discussed?

We like to hear good news, and Moses' message is not good news. It is, however, necessary news. It should be borne in mind that while harshly realistic news may not make people feel good, it is nevertheless the truth, and it needs to be told. Perhaps the Church could actually gain credibility with more people if it was more willing to "tell it like it is" instead of trying so hard to sugarcoat everything in such a way that it seems we are living in denial of the fact of life—which is that it ends in death. This is yet another of the sharp dualities that must mark the Church's message. Life is short, hard, and unfair. You live. You suffer. You die. You are forgotten. Such it is. But life is also the spectacular gift from God, who refuses to allow the legacy of sin to be the final chapter in the story of this world. In spite of life's bitter reality, God will triumph, and the lives of His people will be redeemed and made significant. Both sides of the story must be told with enthusiasm and without holding back.

9. What is God's work that is mentioned in verse 16, and what does that work have to do with the work that we do (v. 17)?

God's "work" is the salvation story that began with creation, continued through Israel, reached its climax in Christ, and will be fulfilled at Christ's second coming. When Moses prays that God's people may see God's work, he is praying that God would hasten the fulfillment of the plan so that we can all see God's unveiled glory revealed in the new creation. But wait—there is more! The prayer is also a request for God to give us eyes to see the progress of God's unfolding story in our own lives and in the lives of those around us. This is the source of much joy. And it is when we see our own labor in the context of God's sweeping plan of redemption that we can delight in our work and realize the value that it has, not intrinsically, but because God works through us and incorporates our work into His overall plan. To be a participant in God's saving activity simply by the faithful doing of our vocations is at once profoundly humbling and wonderfully exciting.

10. In the not-so-distant past, this psalm was considered a standard text to be read at the funerals of Christian people. Do you think the psalm is appropriate to such an occasion? Why do you think that the psalm is no longer used with such regularity? Would it be a good text for a confirmation sermon, or at a wedding?

Perhaps the overall message and impact of the psalm was deemed too sobering or bleak to be used when people were already consumed with grief—a sort of piling on with the Law. Or maybe, people today would rather not be reminded of the reality of their own mortality and the terrifying shortness and futility of life. Whatever the reason, the Church is poorer for the disuse of the psalm. It seems an apt message for virtually any occasion in the life of a believer. What could be more appropriate than to be reminded, in the strongest possible language, of the fundamental reality of life and the place of God within that life? Perhaps God's Word delivers more reality than we can handle!

A Guy's Guide
to Church Lingo

Not everyone can tell a crankshaft from a camshaft, a rooster tail from a red worm, or a divot from a driver. You have to know the lingo (or at least know a mechanic, a bait-and-tackle guy, or a golf pro). Lingo is important, no matter the field, so here are some commonly used Church words and their definitions. Even if you are not already familiar with them, after studying them awhile, you should sound like a pro. Try this: "<u>God</u> has <u>justified</u> me through <u>faith</u> in His Son, <u>Jesus</u> <u>Christ</u>." That wasn't so hard, was it?

–The Editor

Absolve—*to set free from sin*. God absolves us in the Gospel and the Sacraments. Absolution is not merely a symbol. On Christ's behalf, the pastor absolves us after we confess our sins either publicly or privately.

Baptism—*a holy act using water and the Word*. Baptism is not merely a symbol. God truly forgives sins, gives His Holy Spirit, and creates new spiritual life in this Sacrament.

Bible—*God's Word*. There are sixty-six books in the Bible. Because the Holy Spirit inspired each of the Bible's authors to write down every word in the Bible, the Bible is without error.

Christ—*Anointed One* (Greek; in Hebrew: *Messiah*). *Christ* is a title, not Jesus' last name. Jesus is the fulfillment of God's promise to send His Spirit-anointed Son to save us from our sins.

Church—*community of the baptized*. Can also refer to a local congregation or the building in which Christian worship services are held.

Creation—*everything that God our Creator has made*. This includes all planets and stars and satellites, earth, animals, plants, human beings, and spiritual beings we cannot see, such as angels.

Cross—*instrument of torture and death*. By shedding His blood on the cross, Jesus paid the full penalty for our sins and guaranteed that we have God's free and full forgiveness.

Eternal life—*living forever in body and soul in a right relationship with God*. Baptized into Christ, we have God's promise of eternal life, even now in this life.

Faith—*God-given trust in His promises.* Through the Gospel and the Sacraments, God gives us the free gift of faith, which trusts in Jesus alone for salvation.

Forgiveness—*God's act of setting free from the guilt and penalty of sin.* Forgiveness is applied in the Gospel and the Sacraments. Forgiveness is received by all who believe that Jesus is their Savior.

God—*the unseen, almighty, eternal Creator of all that exists.* There is only one God: Father, Son, and Holy Spirit.

Good works—*good deeds.* Ultimately, God performs good works through believers, who are motivated and enabled by His love and forgiveness in Christ. True good works will be rewarded when Jesus returns.

Gospel—*the good news of forgiveness, life, peace, and joy in Jesus.* The Gospel centers on Jesus' incarnation, life, death, resurrection, ascension, and coming again.

Holy Spirit—*Third Person of the Trinity.* Through God's Word, the Holy Spirit guides, convicts, and comforts us with truth that our sins are forgiven for the sake of Jesus.

Jesus—*Son of God and Son of Mary.* Jesus lived, died, rose again from the dead, and ascended into heaven for us. One day He will return in glory for us. Jesus is 100 percent God and 100 percent man, although without sin. See *God.*

Justification—*declared in a right relationship with God.* We are justified through faith in Jesus Christ, our God and Savior.

Law—*what God commands or forbids.* The Law restricts outward behavior (curb), confronts us with our sins (mirror), and shows us how to live God's way (guide).

Lord's Supper—*holy act using bread, wine, and the Word.* Also called Holy Communion; the Eucharist. The Lord's Supper is not merely a symbol. Jesus gives us His true body and His true blood in, with, and under the forms of bread and wine to eat and to drink.

Pastor—literally *"shepherd."* God calls certain men to preach the Gospel and administer the Sacraments in His Church, most usually in a congregation.

Prayer—*communicating with God.* Prayer can be offered alone or with others, out loud privately, using written prayers, or simply from one's heart. God-pleasing prayers are sincere and are based on God's promises in His Word.

Psalms—*a collection of 150 hymns and poems in the Bible.* Written by David, Solomon, and other writers, many psalms were used in the public worship of Israel. Jesus frequently quoted from the Psalms.

Resurrection—*to rise bodily from the dead.* After dying on the cross, Jesus rose from the dead on Easter. When Jesus returns to earth, everyone who has ever lived will be raised from the dead. Those who have trusted in Him will be raised in perfect bodies that will never get sick, grow old, or die.

Sacrament—*holy act instituted by Jesus.* A sacrament is a sacred act instituted by God in which God Himself has joined His Word of promise to a visible element, and by which He offers, gives, and seals the forgiveness of sins earned by Christ. By this definition there are two sacraments: Holy Baptism and the Lord's Supper. Sometimes Holy Absolution is counted as a third sacrament, even though it has no divinely instituted visible element.

Salvation—*deliverance.* To be saved means to be delivered from sin, Satan, and death. Jesus is our Savior; He freely gives us His salvation through the Gospel and the Sacraments.

Sanctification—*to be made holy.* After God declares us holy (justification), He makes us holy (sanctification) through the Gospel and the Sacraments, so that we begin to do good works in His sight.

Sin—*disobedience of God's Law.* Since Adam and Eve, all humans are born under God's condemnation for the sin that dwells within them, which leads them to commit actual sins. The only way to remove the guilt and penalty of sin is through God's forgiveness.

Son of God—*Second Person of the Trinity.* Jesus is both the Son of God and true man, in one person.

Trinity—"*tri-unity,*" *Three in One.* The Father, the Son, and the Holy Spirit are one God. See *God.*

Word—*God's revelation of Himself.* The Bible is God's Word; Jesus, as the Son of God, is God's Word in human flesh.

Worship—*receiving and responding to God's gifts.* God gives us His Word and Sacraments, and we respond to Him with prayers, praise, thanksgiving, offerings, and lives of service.